SIMPLE ASIAN
ONE-POT MEALS

SIMPLE ASIAN
ONE-POT MEALS

80 QUICK, HEALTHY & AFFORDABLE EVERYDAY RECIPES

Ming Tsai & Arthur Boehm

photography by Antonis Achilleos

KYLE BOOKS

For my parents, Iris and Stephen Tsai.
You showed me how to eat, travel, cook,
love, work and live. Most important, you
showed me how to raise children. I'll be
a true success if I can give my children
what you gave me.

M. T.

For Richard Getke, still the best dining
partner.

A. B.

Published in Great Britain in 2011 by
Kyle Books
23 Howland Street, London W1T 4AY
www.kylebooks.com

First published in 2010 by Kyle Books,
an imprint of Kyle Cathie Ltd.
www.kylebooks.com

A CIP catalogue record for this title is
available from the British Library.

ISBN: 978-1-85626-972-8

10 9 8 7 6 5 4 3 2

Ming Tsai is hereby identified as the author
of this work in accordance with section 77
of Copyright, Designs and Patents Act 1988.

Project editor Anja Schmidt
Designer Dirk Kaufman
Photographer Antonis Achilleos
Food styling Ming Tsai
Prop styling Lisa Falso
Copyeditor Janet McDonald
Production Lisa Pinnell and Gemma Jordan

Colour reproduction by Chromagraphics
Printed in Singapore by Tien Wah Press

contents

introduction

I love to cook – but like other busy people, I don't always have time. The chef in me aims to make the best, most excitingly delicious food possible; the dad and home cook in me wants those meals to be prepared hassle free and with the minimum washing-up. The solution? The book you're holding – a collection of 80 fabulous dishes that are cooked, start to finish for the most part, in a single pot.

One-pot cooking began for me at home and was introduced during the fourth season of my Public Television show, 'Simply Ming'. The show's title was chosen because I wanted to present recipes so easy that people would have to try them. That meant using saucepans for sautéing and woks for pasta cooking and braising, among other time-saving techniques. It soon became clear that I had hit upon a great cooking approach to call my own.

Few home cooks have battalions of utensils, and more people might cook at home more often if the process were simplified. While making great meals on the show from less-expensive ingredients like chicken thighs and thin ribs, I also saw that anyone could prepare terrific food more affordably. And, I realised that because I always aim to cook as healthily as possible – yogurt instead of cream, lots of veggies and multigrain ingredients – my one-pot recipes could be better for you. Voila! My one-pot cooking system – and, I hope, a one-pot future for you.

Of course, the pot changes depending on the technique used. The seven methods I've chosen – braise, wok, sauté, roast, high temp, soup and toss – were born for one-pot cooking. They also allow me to present a full range of fabulous dishes, from soups and salads to substantial main courses, that include steamed and flash-fried specialities and everything in between. So much can be achieved in a single pot – you can, for example, prepare a vegetable noodle stir-fry entirely in a wok, from blanching the vegetables and soaking the noodles to their final assembly with other stir-fried ingredients – that you'll marvel at the pot's time-saving versatility. You may even echo my mum, who used to tell me as a young wokking fanatic that the only thing I'd yet to do with that utensil, but probably could, was bathe in it.

No cookbook is gospel. My aim with *Simple Asian One-Pot Meals* is to give you an approach you can make your own so that you can create your unique great one-pot dishes. The easier it is to cook, the more likely you will. You won't have to stop Twittering or sending e-mails – in fact, many of the dishes in the book give you more room to do those things. And you'll enjoy sharing great food made by you more often with those you care about.

Exploring technique through my one-pot system – taking under-utilised woks and saucepans out for a spin – will also help show you how cooking actually works, so you'll be better at it. The proof, though, is always in the eating, and in that regard, I guarantee serious pleasure.

Peace and Good Eating

glossary of ingredients and techniques

Oils and Vinegars

Grapeseed Oil. Taken from grape seeds, this is my oil of choice for sautéing and wok cooking, as it has a light, nutty flavour and relatively high smoke point. I also like to use it in marinades and dressings, as it emulsifies well. It has a clean taste that's superior to other vegetable oils. If you have difficulty finding it, rapeseed oil is a good second choice.

Olive Oil. Most people are familiar with this delicious, healthful product of tree-ripened olives. For the recipes in this book I call for extra-virgin olive oil, the result of the fruit's first, cold pressing. Only 1 per cent acid, it's considered the finest and most flavourful olive oil type. It also ranges widely in colour and fruitiness. The greener oils are usually more robust. Experiment with different oils from different countries until you find those you like best.

Toasted Sesame Oil. I refer to the thick, flavourful, brownish oil made from toasted sesame seeds, which is a staple of the Chinese storecupboard. Unlike refined and almost flavourless sesame oils, which can be used for cooking, this oil is for seasoning only.

Black Vinegar. Similar to balsamic vinegar, this dark, complexly flavoured vinegar is made from glutinous rice and malt. It's used in stir-fried dishes, braises and sauces. Black vinegar hails from the Chinkiang Province of China; it's sometimes labelled 'Chinkiang Vinegar'.

Rice Vinegar. Most commonly a white to golden vinegar with a delicate taste that adds a mild acidity to foods. It should be naturally brewed – check labels. Also check the label to ensure that the vinegar is unseasoned. I prefer organic brands, such as Wan Ja Shan.

Noodles, Rice and Wrappers

Stir-Fry Noodles. Fresh egg and wheat-flour noodles that are used to make chow mein and other dishes. These shouldn't be confused with the crispy noodles that are found in Chinese restaurants and that are often sprinkled on stir-fried dishes. Cooked fresh stir-fry noodles are sometimes formed into a pancake and fried on both sides.

Mung Bean Noodles. Also known as bean thread and cellophane noodles, these fine, translucent noodles are made from ground mung beans, which also supply beansprouts for cooking. The noodles are never cooked, but are instead soaked in hot water until pliable. They're sold dry in packets that range from 25g to 450g.

Ramen. The name refers to an ingredient – Japanese noodles made from wheat flour, salt and water – as well as to commercial noodle-soup kits that contain dehydrated meat, vegetables and flavourings. The noodles, which are sold fresh or dried, usually in Asian food shops, are of course the ingredient of interest here.

Rice Stick Noodles. One of the large family of fresh and dried rice noodles, this thin, flat dried type is widely available in Asian food shops.

Rice Vermicelli. Relatively long, thin, round rice noodles, these take their name from the Italian pasta called 'little worms' in English. They're often sold in 450g or 500g packets.

Shanghai Noodles. Sold both fresh and dried, these medium-thin egg noodles are often available in 340g packets. If unavailable, substitute any medium egg noodles or thick dried or fresh spaghetti.

Soba Noodles. These earthy buckwheat noodles are probably the most famous of all Japanese pasta, traditionally served in soups or cold with a dipping sauce made with dashi and soy sauce. There are also flavoured types of soba noodles – my favourite is cha soba, which has the colour and flavour of green tea.

Sushi Rice. A short-grained rice that, when cooked, has a moderately sticky texture that is perfect for making sushi. Sushi rice labelling is sometimes inexact; it's often called 'Japanese rice', for example. The most highly regarded sushi rice is koshihikari. Like risotto rices, it maintains a chewy firmness when cooked, making it perfect for sushi – as well as for risottos.

Wonton Noodles. Thin wheat noodles that take their name from the wonton soup in which they traditionally appear, these are sold fresh and dried.

Wonton Wrappers. Made from flour, eggs and salt, the wrappers come in a variety of forms, round and square, thick and thin. Wontons need round wrappers; square is the choice for making ravioli. In either case, I recommend the thinnest wrappers you can find, which come in packets usually labelled 'extra thin'. They last refrigerated for about a week, and frozen for up to two months.

Seasonings, Condiments and Aromatics

Fermented Black Beans. A staple of the Chinese storecupboard, this pungent ingredient is made from soya beans that are partially decomposed, dried and usually salted. Sold most often in plastic bags, the beans last indefinitely if stored airtight in a cool, lightless place. The beans should be rinsed before using to remove excess salt.

Five-Spice Powder. A traditional Chinese seasoning blend usually made from equal parts of ground cinnamon, cloves, star anise, fennel seeds and Szechuan peppercorns. It has a fragrant 'warm-cool' flavour and an affinity for fatty meats such as pork and duck. Since the number five is considered significant in Chinese belief, this spice is thought to be health-promoting.

Fish Sauce. This Southeast Asian staple, called *nam pla* in Thailand and *noc mam* in Vietnam, is made from salted and fermented anchovies and is used as often as the Chinese use soy sauce. I prefer the Thai Three Crab brand, which has a clean sea taste and less sweetness than other brands I've tried. Once opened, keep fish sauce in the fridge.

Hoisin Sauce. Sweet and spicy, this traditional soya bean-based Chinese ingredient and condiment can also contain sugar, garlic and vinegar, depending on the brand. Once opened, keep the sauce refrigerated.

Kimchi. This hot, extremely pungent condiment is a staple of the Korean table. Made from fermented vegetables, usually cabbage, kimchi will last indefinitely in its pot or jar, refrigerated.

Korean Red Chilli Flakes. Known as *gochugalu* in Korean, this fiery ingredient is made from sun-dried thin chillies. Available in Asian food shops, store it airtight in the refrigerator or freezer.

Mirin. An essential ingredient in Japanese cooking, mirin is rice wine with sugar. It adds delicate sweetness to many dishes and is also used, traditionally, to glaze foods. I recommend hon-mirin, which is naturally brewed and contains natural sugars, rather than aji-mirin, which can contain sweeteners.

Miso. The primary ingredient in the Japanese soup from which it takes its name, miso is a savoury paste made from soya beans, rice and barley or brown beans. For the recipes in this book, I call for shiro miso, sometimes called white miso, which is rice-based. Available in cans, jars and tubs, miso is best stored in the fridge, where it lasts up to three months.

Ponzu. A thin citrus-based sauce commonly used in Japanese cooking, ponzu is traditionally made from mirin, rice vinegar, katsuobushi flakes – dried fermented tuna – and seaweed. I use a naturally brewed wheat-free, tamari-based ponzu made by Wan Ja Shan.

Rock Sugar. A traditional Chinese ingredient, rock sugar has a richer, more mellow flavour than ordinary refined white sugars. As the name suggests, the sugar, which comes in plastic bags, consists of large lumps that keep indefinitely if stored in a cool, dry place. Rock sugar not only sweetens but gives a sheen to sauces or braising liquids.

Sambal. A fiery Southeast Asian chilli-based condiment, the type I call for, and which you're most likely to find, is sambal olek. Made from chillies, vinegar and salt, it contains one of the additives such as garlic or shrimp paste that some other sambal types do have.

Soy Sauce. The essential Chinese seasoning, soy sauce has been used for more than three thousand years. I call for 'regular' soy sauce, which is often called 'light' or sometimes 'thin' to distinguish it from 'dark' or thicker kinds. Soy sauce is made from a soya bean flour and water mixture, which should be naturally fermented or brewed, rather than synthetically or chemically manufactured. Look for 'naturally brewed' on the label and read the ingredient listings. Avoid soy sauces that contain hydrolysed soya protein, corn syrup and caramel colour – a sure sign of an ersatz sauce. Japanese Kikkoman soy sauce is a standby, but I prefer an organic brand like Wan Ja Shan.

Tamari Sauce. A traditional soya bean-based Japanese seasoning sometimes confused with soy sauce but darker and richer. I call for wheat-free tamari, sometimes labelled as 'organic, wheat-free', which I prefer for its good pure taste. Check ingredient lists on the labels to assure yourself of a wheat-free product. Wan Ja Shan is my brand of choice.

Togarashi. These Japanese chillies are available fresh or dried, and also dried and ground. The latter is the kind required for the recipes in this book and can be found in bottles in Asian food shops.

Vegetarian Oyster Sauce. Traditional oyster sauce is a versatile ingredient made from fresh oysters that are cooked and seasoned with soy sauce, salt and spices. Though its somewhat 'fishy' taste dissipates in cooking, some people would rather forgo oysters entirely. For them, I recommend vegetarian oyster sauce, which relies on shiitake mush-rooms in place of oysters – a reasonable substitution, as both are *umami* rich. I prefer the Wan Ja Shan brand.

Yuzu Juice. Squeezed from a sour Japanese citrus fruit used primarily for its rind, the yuzu juice has a tart flavour that is reminiscent of lemon and limes. It makes a delicious addition to marinades and dressings.

Other Ingredients

Chicken Sausages. Alternatives to a traditional pork-based sausage can be disappointing. But if you buy a quality product, you'll be rewarded with a tasty sausage that's sometimes hard to tell from more traditional kinds.

Coconut Milk. Used traditionally in Southeast Asian rice desserts, curries and shellfish recipes, coconut milk is made by steeping freshly grated coconut in boiling water or milk. I like to use it not only for its flavour but for its richness; it is a flavourful alternative to double cream in many recipes. Coconut milk spoils quickly, so freeze any unused quantity.

Edamame. Young green Japanese soya beans, sold in the pod or shelled in packets, fresh or frozen. The shelled beans add a delicious creamy crunchiness to dishes. Fresh beans are available in Japanese and some other Asian food shops usually from June to October.

Rice crisps. These are great for enjoying as a light snack or as an accompaniment to dishes. They're available in a variety of different flavours.

Panko. These flaky Japanese bread-crumbs are used primarily to coat foods for frying. Their texture yields a more delicate crust than their Western counter-parts. Panko is available in cellophane bags, in which it lasts indefinitely. Once opened, freeze any unused quantity.

Preserved Lemons. A standard ingredient and condiment of North Africa, these are lemons pickled briefly in a salt and lemon juice mixture. Find them in jars in speciality food shops or online.

Shaoxing Wine. Named after the city of its original manufacture, this pre-eminent Chinese rice wine has been in production for millennia. Often sold in ceramic containers, the wine is both drunk and used in recipes. Its taste is similar to that of sherry, which can be substituted for it.

Tofu. Prepared from curdled soya milk in a process similar to cheese making, tofu is an ancient Chinese and Japanese product that comes in extra-firm, firm, soft and silken styles. Silken tofu is the most delicate, even if labelled 'firm'. Rich in protein and low in fat and cholesterol, tofu is extremely nutritious. Though sold fresh in water, it is most commonly available in packets or tubs. Unused portions should be refrigerated in the original container or transferred to water, which should be changed daily.

Techniques and Other Matters

Brining. I always brine pork before cooking it, as well as chicken and turkey for Thanksgiving or Christmas, and recommend that you do too. Brining – soaking meat or poultry in a solution of salt, water and usually sugar – greatly improves taste and juiciness. It works because the brined item absorbs the solution and retains it during cooking. Brining formulas and instructions appear in the recipes.

Deglazing. The process by which a small amount of liquid, often wine, is added to pans in which food has been sautéed and then removed. The liquid is stirred to incorporate the flavourful caramelised crust on the pan's base. Other liquids may then be added.

Food Allergies. Work smart. To avoid potential allergic reactions, always clean your chopping board between jobs. If, for example, I'm chopping peanuts or other nuts, I reflexively wash my board before chopping another ingredient on the same surface. Keeping your board clean in this manner also avoids cross-contamination – the transfer of bacteria from raw ingredients to cooked ones. This is especially important when you're having guests whose food sensitivities you – or they – might not know.

Heating the Pan Before Adding Oil. To minimise the possibility of sticking, all my recipes direct that a pan used for browning be heated before adding oil. Following this method, the oil is in contact with the pan for less time and is thus less likely to break down – to become viscous and gummy and thus sticky. Even a little broken-down oil can contribute to sticking.

Making Rice. For perfectly cooked rice, I recommend using a rice maker, as millions of Asians do. You get flawless rice every time – and the rice can be held hot in the cooker for up to 8 hours. For making white or brown rice or a combination on the hob, I always follow the 'Mt Fuji' method, which involves using your hand to determine how much water is needed in relation to the rice (see 50-50 White and Brown Rice for 4 Servings).

Cooked Rice

50-50 White and Brown Rice for 4 Servings. Rinse 280g brown rice, and soak it in fresh cold water to cover for 1 hour. Drain and transfer the rice to a medium saucepan.

Place 280g white rice in a large bowl in the sink. Rinse the rice by filling the bowl with cold water and stirring the rice with a hand. Drain and repeat until the water in the bowl is clear. Transfer the rice to the saucepan.

Flatten the rice with your palm and, without removing it, add water until it touches the highest knuckle of your middle finger. Cover and boil over a high heat for 10 minutes. Reduce the heat to medium and simmer the rice for 30 minutes. Turn off the heat and leave the rice to stand, covered, for 20 minutes to plump up. Stir gently and serve.

For about 490g Wild Rice. Place 160g wild rice in a large bowl in the sink. Rinse the rice by filling the bowl with cold water and stirring the rice with a hand. Drain and repeat until the water in the bowl is clear of any debris. Bring 700ml water to the boil in a saucepan, add the rice, reduce the heat and simmer for 35–55 minutes until the rice is tender – depending on the rice. (Check for tenderness periodically.) Stir and serve.

Organic Poultry and Meat. I always recommend that cooks seek out meat and poultry that's certified organic – or is labelled in such a way to indicate that the animal has been raised and slaughtered humanely, without antibiotics or growth-promotants, and on wholesome feed. In the case of poultry, I specify that the birds be free-range. Because of the care given to poultry destined for the kosher table, I also recommend kosher chicken and meat products. If you can, buy meat and poultry that's been locally raised and processed by small producers, which are usually more conscientious about animal welfare than mass-manufacturers. The pay-off for such choosiness is better, more healthful and flavourful, eating.

Roll-Cutting. A traditional Chinese technique that ensures maximum exposed surface area so that cylindrical vegetables like carrots or asparagus cook quickly when stir-fried. Roll-cut vegetables also look pretty. To roll-cut, first slice away the stem end on an angle. Roll the vegetable about a quarter turn away from you and slice again at the same angle, about 4cm further down or to the length that the recipe specifies. Continue rolling and slicing until the vegetable has been entirely cut.

Seasoning. I call for frequent seasoning adjustment, as necessary – 'correcting' salt, pepper and other seasonings as you cook. To do this, you must taste a dish again and again as it cooks. Repeated tasting is basic to ensuring a delicious result. Please understand that I don't advise overloading a dish with one seasoning or another, but rather bringing it to its maximum flavour potential through judicial seasoning adjustment.

Skimming Surface Fat with a Ladle. First, using the ladle, remove the larger quantity of surface fat from stocks or soups, transferring the fat to a bowl. Continue to skim; the ladle will now contain less fat and some stock. Allow the fat to rise to the surface and circle the ladle gently over the bowl, permitting the fat to spill into it. Return the remaining stock to the soup. Repeat until all fat is removed.

1

Braising is the original one-pot, 'set-it-and-forget-it' technique. To braise, all you do is brown meat or poultry in a pot, add seasonings, aromatics and liquid, and simmer until the main item is done. You then go about your business while the house fills with the best possible cooking smells – throw away those scented candles! A few hours later you've got meltingly tender food.

Easy as they are to do, though, successful braises require great texture-flavour play-offs, and I've made sure all the braises here get them. Luscious, tangy Pork Belly with Jalapeño-Pineapple Salsa and chilli-fired Thin Ribs with Root Vegetables are delectable examples.

Braising also brings one-pot ease to cooking less-expensive cuts of meat, like lamb shanks or oxtail, which require long simmering to be tender. The reward – see Oxtails with Shiitakes and Quinoa – is simply supremely succulent dining. And braising is flexible; enjoy your braised dish today, then store any leftovers for later. They'll be just as delicious, if not better, the next day.

BRAISE

star anise-ginger 'braised' whole chicken

TO DRINK:
A crisp new-world Sauvignon Blanc, like Craggy Range 'Te Muna Road' from New Zealand

I often wonder why people cook chicken by any other method than this traditional Chinese one, technically a poach-braise. It delivers beautifully tender, silky meat – and it couldn't be easier. All you do is put a chicken in a pot with stock and flavourings, simmer it until it's partially cooked, then remove it from the heat. The bird finishes cooking in the hot liquid, and emerges perfectly done. The chicken's almost fat-free, having left most of its fat in the stock. Serve with crusty bread.

1. In a tall, wide saucepan or large flameproof casserole dish, combine the celery, carrots, onions, peppercorns, bay leaves, thyme, parsley, star anise, ginger and soy sauce. And the stock and season with salt and pepper.

2. Season the chicken inside and out with salt and pepper. Add the chicken to the pot breast side up. It should be completely covered with stock, but if not, add more.

3. Cover and bring just to a simmer over a medium-high heat. Reduce the heat to low and barely simmer for 45 minutes. Turn off the heat and leave to stand, covered, for 30 minutes–1 hour (the chicken won't cook any further after 30 minutes). Remove the chicken and strain the broth, reserving the vegetables. Carve the chicken and serve with the vegetables and bowls of the broth.

[Serves 4]

4 celery sticks, cut into 1cm pieces

2 large carrots, peeled and roll-cut into 1cm pieces (see page 13) or cut conventionally

2 large onions, cut into 1cm dice

1 teaspoon black peppercorns

2 bay leaves

2 sprigs fresh thyme

¼ bunch fresh flat-leaf parsley

2 star anise

2 tablespoons finely chopped fresh ginger

125ml naturally brewed soy sauce or wheat-free tamari sauce

1.9 litres fresh chicken stock or stock made from low-salt chicken stock cubes, plus extra if needed

sea salt and freshly ground black pepper

one 2.25–2.7kg whole chicken, wing tips folded over the back

TO DRINK:
A fruity, bright Pinot Noir, like
Robert Mondavi Winery or Domaine
Chandon Carneros from California

[Serves 4]

BRAISING SAUCE

950ml naturally brewed soy sauce

475ml good red wine

900g rock sugar (see page 10)

**7.5cm piece of unpeeled fresh ginger,
washed and cut into 5mm slices**

3 dried bird's eye chillies

**1 medium head garlic, halved
horizontally**

1 star anise

**1 bunch spring onions, white and greens
parts, cut into 7.5cm lengths**

**1 medium unpeeled orange,
washed and quartered**

2 cinnamon sticks

–

10 duck legs (with thighs)

**1 large sweet potato, peeled and cut into
1cm slices**

**1 large daikon, peeled and cut into 1cm
slices**

–

**50-50 White and Brown Rice (see page 12),
for serving**

red-roast duck legs with sweet potatoes and daikon

This incredibly savoury braise – and it's a braise, despite its name – takes me back to my childhood, when the scent of simmering red-roast dishes perfumed our house so invitingly. Whole ducks are often used for red-roast dishes, but this one features convenient duck legs – legs with thighs, actually – that you can get cheap at Asian food shops, from butchers or online. The sweetness of the potatoes is a perfect foil for the chillies' heat, and the daikon adds crunch. I love this dish served with sambal used as a condiment and a 50-50 mixture of brown and white rice.

1. In a large non-reactive saucepan, combine all the braising sauce ingredients. Add 700ml water and bring to the boil over a high heat. Reduce the heat and simmer for 15–20 minutes until the sugar dissolves. Taste and add more soy sauce if the flavour lacks depth, or more water if the sauce seems too seasoned.

2. Add the duck legs and simmer for about 2^1/$_2$ hours until the meat falls from the bones. (**Quick Tip**: You can use a pressure cooker to do this. Cook the duck under pressure for 45 minutes, release the pressure, uncover and proceed as follows.) Twenty minutes before the duck is cooked, add the potatoes and daikon. Test the potatoes with a fork to make sure they're tender; if not, simmer a bit longer.

3. Remove the legs and vegetables and keep warm. Skim the cooking sauce (a ladle is good for this, see page 13). Divide the duck legs and vegetables between four individual plates, spoon sauce over them and serve with the rice.

Ming's Tip:
Strain and freeze any extra sauce for future braises of chicken or pork shoulder. The skimmed fat should also be stored, refrigerated. It's great for searing meats or for making scrambled eggs.

oxtail and shiitakes with quinoa

The Chinese love oxtail, a cut that is insufficiently enjoyed in the West. Given a slow braise, oxtail is deliciously unctuous eating. Here, I pair it with shiitakes, for earthiness and texture, and serve it on quinoa, which, if you haven't tried it, is similar in texture to couscous, but is even better for you. When my wife Polly is sick, she always requests this dish. The Chinese believe oxtail has medicinal properties, but Polly loves it for its soul-satisfying tastiness.

1. Fill a medium bowl with warm water. Add the shiitakes and soak them for 30 minutes–1 hour until soft. Drain and discard the stems. Quarter the large caps and halve the smaller ones. Set aside.

2. In a large shallow plate, combine the flour and paprika. Season the oxtail pieces with salt and pepper, and dredge in the flour mixture.

3. Heat a tall, wide saucepan over a medium heat. Add 2 tablespoons of the oil and swirl to coat the bottom. When the oil is hot, add the oxtail pieces, in batches, if necessary. Cook the oxtail, turning once, for about 8 minutes until browned. Set the oxtail aside.

4. Add the remaining tablespoon of oil to the pan and swirl. When the oil is hot, add the onions and garlic, season with salt and pepper and sauté for about 3 minutes until softened. Add the wine, deglaze the pan and simmer for about 2 minutes to reduce the liquid by half. Add the reserved mushrooms and the bamboo shoots, season with salt and pepper and return the oxtail to the pan. Add the soy sauce and enough water to cover the ingredients. Adjust the seasoning, if necessary. Bring to a simmer, cover and cook over a medium-high heat for 2–3 hours until the meat is falling off the bone. (**Quick Tip:** cook in a pressure cooker, over a medium-high heat, for 1 hour.)

5. Meanwhile, make the quinoa. In a large saucepan, combine the quinoa and 475ml water. Bring to the boil, reduce the heat and simmer, stirring occasionally, for 12–14 minutes until the water is absorbed.

6. Transfer the quinoa to a large bowl, top with the oxtail mixture and serve.

TO DRINK:
A big Spanish red, like Borsao Tres Picos Garnacha

[Serves 4]

30g dried shiitakes

240g white or brown rice flour

1 tablespoon paprika

6 large oxtail pieces (175–225g each)

sea salt and freshly ground black pepper

3 tablespoons grapeseed or rapeseed oil

2 onions, cut into 2.5cm dice

2 tablespoons finely chopped garlic

225ml Shaoxing wine or dry sherry

one 350g can whole bamboo shoots, rinsed well, cut into 2.5cm lengths

3 tablespoons naturally brewed soy sauce

170g quinoa

Ming's Tip:
When transferring the oxtail from the pan to a serving bowl, be careful to keep the meat and bones together.

aromatic thin ribs with root vegetables

TO DRINK:
A big red wine, like a `Black Label'
Shiraz from Australia

[Serves 4]

215g plain flour

1 tablespoon chilli powder

6 single-rib thin ribs or 3 double-rib

sea salt and freshly ground black pepper

3 tablespoons grapeseed or rapeseed oil

2 onions, cut into 2.5cm dice

2 tablespoons finely chopped garlic

450g trimmed baby carrots, or peeled regular carrots, cut into chunks

6 celery sticks, split lengthways and halved if large

1 celeriac, peeled and cut into 2.5cm dice

1 large sweet potato, cut into 2.5cm dice

1 large parsnip, roll-cut into 2.5cm pieces (see page 13) or cut conventionally

2 tablespoons naturally brewed soy sauce

I live in New England, and when the frost builds up on the windows, I make this stick-to-the-ribs (no pun!) dish. It's full of good things – chewy thin ribs and sweet root vegetables cooked until their flavours meld into a deeply delicious whole. It's also easy to do: once everything's in the pot, you can forget about the dish until it's time to eat, which, trust me, you'll definitely want to do. Serve this with crusty bread for sauce-mopping.

1. In a large shallow plate, combine the flour and chilli powder. Season the ribs with salt and pepper and dredge in the flour mixture.

2. Heat a tall, wide saucepan over a medium heat. Add 2 tablespoons of the oil and swirl to coat the bottom. When the oil is hot, shake the excess flour mixture from the ribs, add them to the pan and cook, turning once, for about 8 minutes until browned. Set the ribs aside.

3. Add the remaining oil to the pan and swirl to coat the bottom. When the oil is hot, add the onions and garlic and sauté, stirring, for about 3 minutes. Add the carrots, celery, celeriac, potato and parsnip. Season with salt and pepper. Add the ribs, soy sauce and enough water to almost cover the ingredients. Taste and adjust the seasoning, if necessary. Cover and cook over a medium heat for about 3 hours until a paring knife passes through the meat easily. (*Quick Tip*: cook in a pressure cooker, over a medium-high heat, for 1 hour.) Transfer the ribs and vegetables to a large bowl and serve.

curry beef with potatoes and onions

TO DRINK:
A California red blend, like Elderton Ashmead Cabernet Sauvignon

[Serves 4]

900g braising steak, cut into 2.5cm cubes

sea salt and freshly ground black pepper

3 tablespoons grapeseed or rapeseed oil

2 large onions, cut into 2.5cm dice

1 tablespoon finely chopped fresh ginger

2 tablespoons Madras curry powder

2 large unpeeled Maris Piper, Desiree or King Edward potatoes, washed and cut into 2.5cm dice (see Ming's Tip)

950ml fresh chicken stock or stock made from low-salt chicken stock cubes

1 lemon, cut into wedges

–

50-50 White and Brown Rice (see page 12), for serving

The Japanese love beef curry dishes, which I'm always happy to sample when I'm in Japan. The curries vary in heat and are usually served on rice. My easy version features tasty (and relatively inexpensive) braising steak, plus onions and potatoes, which absorb the delicious braising liquid. I also call for Madras curry powder, which I find the most reliably – and subtly – flavourful. If you're a curry fan, this quickly made version will do the trick.

1. Season the meat with salt and pepper. Heat a tall, wide saucepan over a high heat. Add 2 tablespoons of the oil and swirl to coat the bottom. When the oil is hot, add the beef, in batches if necessary. Sauté for about 3 minutes until browned on both sides. Remove and set aside.

2. Reduce the heat to medium-high and add the remaining tablespoon of oil. Swirl, and when the oil is hot, add the onions, ginger and curry powder. Sauté, stirring, for about 2 minutes until softened. Add the potatoes, the meat and the chicken stock and adjust the seasoning, if necessary. Bring to a simmer, cover and cook for about 1¾ hours until the meat is spoon-tender.

3. Place the rice on a platter or distribute between four individual plates. Top with the beef and vegetables, garnish with the lemon wedges and serve.

Ming's Tip:

To dice the potatoes, peel and make a square block of each by trimming the top, bottom and sides, six cuts in all. Slice the potatoes lengthways to make planks, pile the planks and slice lengthways again. Cut widthways to dice.

orange-ginger lamb shanks with barley

Every time I eat barley I wonder why it's not more popular. It's delicious – particularly in this hearty dish, where its chewy nuttiness partners with the lamb perfectly. (I won't mention that barley's good for you too – or have I just?) Orange and ginger brighten the dish, which also makes a great presentation. I serve this often for meat-loving friends, and I suggest you do too.

1. In a large saucepan, cook the barley in an ample quantity of boiling water for about 45 minutes until tender. Using a large sieve, drain the barley, then run cold tap water through it until it's cold. Drain and set aside at room temperature.

2. Meanwhile, season the lamb shanks with salt and pepper. Heat a saucepan over a medium-high heat, add the oil, and when hot, add the lamb. Cook on all sides for 8–10 minutes until browned. Transfer to a plate.

3. Add the onions, carrots and celery to the pan, season with salt and pepper and cook, stirring, for about 3 minutes until the vegetables have softened. Add the wine, deglaze the pan and simmer for about 8 minutes until the wine is reduced by about a quarter. Add the orange quarters, soy sauce, brown sugar, ginger and chillies. Return the lamb shanks to the pan and add enough water to barely cover them. Season with salt and pepper. Bring the liquid to a simmer, cover and reduce the heat to low. Cook for about 3 hours until the meat is falling off the bones.

4. Mound the barley on four individual serving plates or a platter. Top with the lamb, spoon the braising liquid over, garnish with the orange slices and serve.

TO DRINK:
A Bordeaux blend, like Château Cantemerle, Haut Médoc, France

[Serves 4]

400g pearl barley

4 lamb shanks (about 1.8kg), preferably from the hind legs

sea salt and freshly ground black pepper

2 tablespoons grapeseed or rapeseed oil

2 large onions, roughly chopped

3 carrots, peeled and roughly chopped

3 celery sticks, roughly chopped

1 bottle dry red wine

5 large oranges, 4 quartered, one cut into 5mm slices, for garnish

125ml naturally brewed soy sauce

200g soft dark brown sugar

four 5mm slices unpeeled fresh ginger, cut lengthways from a 5–10cm piece

3 dried bird's eye chillies

Ming's Tip:
Try to get hind-leg shanks, which are meatier than those from the forelegs.

garlic osso buco with celeriac

Osso buco – braised veal shank – is a much-loved Italian speciality. My version honours the traditional recipe, including its use of garlic, which I've added copiously (forewarned is forearmed, though cooking mellows its flavour), and is of course tilted towards the East. I've also added celeriac, an underappreciated vegetable, for its special, earthy flavour. This is so good I recommend making a double batch and freezing half for later enjoyment. Crusty bread completes the feast.

1. In a large shallow plate, combine the flour and chilli powder. Season the osso buco with salt and pepper. Dredge in the flour mixture and set aside.

2. Heat a tall, wide saucepan over a medium heat. Add 2 tablespoons of the oil and swirl to coat the bottom. When the oil is hot, add the osso buco, in batches if necessary, and cook, turning once, for about 8 minutes until browned. Remove the osso buco and set aside.

3. Add the remaining oil, swirl, and when hot, add the onions and garlic. Season with salt and pepper and sauté for about 1 minute until slightly softened. Add the carrots and celery, season with salt and pepper and sauté for 1–2 minutes. Add the wine and cook for 2–3 minutes until reduced the by half. Return the osso buco to the pan and add the soy sauce, thyme and enough water to cover the ingredients. Season with salt and pepper, cover and simmer for about 3 hours until the meat falls from the bone. (**Quick Tip**: cook in a pressure cooker, over a medium-high heat, for 1 hour.) Add the celeriac and cook for 15–20 minutes until soft. Transfer the vegetables to a platter or four individual plates, top with the osso buco and its sauce and serve.

TO DRINK:
A big red wine, like Duckhorn Wine Company Paraduxx Zinfandel from California

[Serves 4]

215g plain flour

1 tablespoon chilli powder

6 large osso buco, each about 5cm thick

sea salt and freshly ground black pepper

3 tablespoons grapeseed or rapeseed oil

2 onions, cut into 2.5cm dice

20 garlic cloves, thinly sliced

450g trimmed baby carrots, or peeled regular carrots, cut into chunks

4 celery sticks, cut into 2.5cm dice

475ml red wine

4 tablespoons naturally brewed soy sauce

3 sprigs fresh thyme

2 large celeriac, cut into 1cm dice

Ming's Tip:
I call for six shank sections because people always want seconds.

TO DRINK:
Dow's Ten Year Old Tawny Port

[Serves 4]

350ml naturally brewed soy sauce

100g soft dark brown sugar

225ml of the recommended port (see To Drink) or similar

6 thin slices washed and unpeeled fresh ginger, cut lengthways from a 5–10cm piece

10 garlic cloves, crushed

2 bunches spring onions, white and green parts, 3 pieces thinly sliced, the rest cut into 5cm lengths

2 cinnamon sticks

sea salt and freshly ground black pepper

900g pork belly, cut into 5cm cubes

315g fresh pineapple, cut into 5mm dice

1 jalapeño chilli, stems discarded and finely chopped, seeds included

pork belly with jalapeño-pineapple salsa

Pork belly has become all the rage, but it's long been adored in China, where it's braised until silky. Here, its richness is offset by hot and tangy salsa – the perfect accompaniment. Also important to this dish's exceptional flavourfulness is port, whose sweetness enhances that of the meat. And garlic lovers will also rejoice at first taste. This is great served as a starter or as a light main course.

1. In a tall, wide saucepan, combine the soy sauce, sugar, port, ginger, garlic, spring onion lengths and cinnamon sticks. Bring to a simmer over a medium heat and season with salt and pepper.

2. Transfer the pork to the pan and add enough water to cover. Simmer, covered, for about 2 hours until the pork is cooked through. (*Quick Tip*: cook in a pressure cooker, over a medium-high heat, for 40 minutes.)

3. Meanwhile, make the salsa. In a small bowl, combine the pineapple, sliced spring onions and jalapeño and season with salt and pepper. Divide the salsa between four individual serving plates, reserving some for garnishing. Top with the pork, garnish with the remaining salsa, spoon the braising liquid around the pork and serve.

2

The wok is an amazing cooking tool – *the* one-pot wonder. A utensil of many uses, it's peerless for creating maximally flavoured meals in minutes. Folklore has it that the wok originated when Genghis Khan used his inverted helmet as a cooking vessel. It's certain that it was invented in East Asia, where cooking fuel was in short supply and portable cooking tools were obligatory. The wok's 'secret' is its round-bottomed shape, which allows very hot seasoned oil to puddle at its base, permitting quick cooking as stir-fried ingredients pass through it repeatedly. This high-heat technique ensures food of vivid colour and taste. And your dish is ready in minutes.

A wok was the first pot I ever cooked with. I soon learned it could be used not only for stir-frying but for braising, steaming – even for pasta cooking. Sometimes combining these methods to make a single dish, recipes in this chapter, such as Green Peppercorn Beef with Asparagus and Rotini and Pork Kimchi with Noodles, show how deeply convenient, as well as delicious, wok cooking is.

WOK

chicken and tri-pepper chow mein

Growing up, my dad would open the fridge, pull out a few ingredients and get a chow mein on the table in about 15 minutes. Peppers were almost always a part of these dishes, and I celebrate them – and him – in this quick and easy stir-fry. Chicken, a touch of honey and fresh lime juice are also key to the deliciousness of this easy dish.

1. Fill a large bowl with water and add ice cubes. In a wok, cook the noodles in abundant boiling salted water until al dente: 3 minutes if fresh, 8–10 minutes if dried or according to the packet instructions. Drain and transfer the noodles to the iced water. When the noodles are cold, drain, transfer to a plate, coat lightly with oil and set aside.

2. Drain the wok, dry it and heat over a high heat. Add 4 tablespoons of the oil and swirl to coat the pan. When the oil is hot, add the chicken and stir-fry for about 6 minutes until the chicken is cooked through. Transfer to a plate.

3. Add the remaining 2 tablespoons oil to the wok, swirl, and when hot, add the garlic, ginger and spring onions. Stir-fry for about 1 minute until soft. Add the soy sauce, deglaze the wok and add the honey and lime juice. Simmer for about 30 seconds until the liquid is reduced by one quarter. Return the chicken with any juice on the plate to the wok and add the peppers. Toss, add the noodles and heat through for about 2 minutes.

4. Transfer to a platter, drizzle with the sesame oil and serve.

TO DRINK:
An Austrian white wine, like Weingut Huber Alte Setzen Gruner Veltliner

[Serves 4]

ice cubes

225g fresh or dried stir-fry or Shanghai noodles

sea salt

6 tablespoons grapeseed or rapeseed oil, plus more for coating the noodles

675g boneless, skinless chicken breasts, cut across the width into 8mm strips

3 tablespoons finely chopped garlic

2 tablespoons finely chopped fresh ginger

1 bunch spring onions, white and green parts, cut into 2.5cm lengths

4 tablespoons naturally brewed soy sauce

85g honey

juice of 2 limes

3 small peppers, red, green and yellow, deseeded and cut into 2.5cm dice

1 tablespoon toasted sesame oil, for drizzling

TO DRINK:
A light India pale ale, like Greene King IPA

[Serves 4]

1 tablespoon sugar

2 tablespoons sambal

4 tablespoons naturally brewed soy sauce

1 tablespoon toasted sesame oil

grated zest and juice of 1 lemon

900g uncooked dark chicken meat (from the legs and/or thighs), cut into 1cm dice

30g cornflour

sea salt and freshly ground black pepper

5 tablespoons grapeseed or rapeseed oil

3 tablespoons finely chopped garlic

2 tablespoons finely chopped fresh ginger

1 teaspoon coarsely ground Szechuan peppercorns (see Ming's Tip)

250g trimmed baby carrots, sliced 5mm thick

5 celery sticks, cut into 1cm dice

150g unsalted roasted peanuts

–

50-50 White and Brown Rice, for serving (see page 12)

Ming's Tip:

Before grinding the Szechuan peppercorns, sieve them to ensure that any twigs or small pebbles are removed.

kung pao chicken with house rice

In Szechuan, their place of origin, kung pao dishes always contain chillies and Szechuan peppercorns. Western versions, usually made with chicken, omit the peppercorns and always include peanuts. My version has the best of both worlds. I use chicken – flavourful dark meat – plus peanuts and the peppercorns, which the Chinese say produce *mala*, an intriguing, tingly numbness on the tongue. Lemon juice adds bracing acidity to this new old favourite.

1. In a small bowl, combine the sugar, sambal, soy sauce, sesame oil and lemon zest and juice and stir to dissolve the sugar. Set aside.

2. In a large bowl, combine the chicken and cornflour, and season with salt and pepper. Toss the chicken to coat it lightly in the cornflour, remove the chicken to a plate and set it aside.

3. Heat a wok over a high heat. Add 2 tablespoons of the oil and swirl to coat the pan. When the oil is hot, add half the chicken and stir-fry, separating the pieces, for 3–4 minutes until the chicken is cooked through. Transfer the chicken to a plate, add 2 more tablespoons of the oil, swirl, and when the oil is hot, stir-fry the remaining chicken. Transfer the chicken to the plate.

4. Add the remaining tablespoon of oil and swirl. When the oil is hot, add the garlic, ginger and peppercorns and stir-fry for about 30 seconds until softened. Add the carrots, celery and peanuts and stir-fry for about 2 minutes until the flavours have combined. Add the sugar mixture, and when it simmers, return the chicken to the pan. Stir to combine.

5. Make a bed of the rice on a platter, top with the stir-fry and serve.

beef, shiitake and broccoli stir-fry

Stir-fried beef with broccoli is a great Chinese dish that can, however, miss the mark. I've made sure this version is excitingly flavoured – and it features shiitakes. This makes a completely satisfying family meal that's quick to put together once the beef has been left to marinate. The natural accompaniment here is my 50-50 White and Brown Rice.

1. In a large resalable plastic bag, combine the steak, ginger, garlic, spring onions and oyster sauce. Seal the bag and use your hands to distribute the ingredients. Marinate, refrigerated, for at least I hour and up to 5 hours.

2. Meanwhile, separate the broccoli into florets. Cut off their long stems and, using a chef's knife, square the stems so that they resemble elongated blocks. Cut the stems lengthways into 5mm pieces, then stack them and cut lengthways into 5mm strips.

3. Fill a large bowl with water and add ice cubes. Fill a wok with water and bring to the boil. Add the broccoli and blanch for 30 seconds. Drain the broccoli and transfer it to the bowl. When the broccoli is cold, drain and set aside.

4. Heat the wok over a high heat. Add 2 tablespoons of the oil and swirl to coat the pan. When the oil is hot, add the mushrooms and stir-fry for about 2 minutes until soft. Season with salt and pepper and transfer the mushrooms to a plate. Add 2 more tablespoons of the oil and swirl to coat the pan. When the oil is hot, add half the beef and stir-fry for 5–6 minutes until medium-rare. Using a skimmer, transfer the beef to the plate with the mushrooms. Add the remaining oil, swirl to coat the pan, add the remaining beef and stir-fry until done. Return the reserved beef and mushrooms to the wok, add the broccoli and stock and heat through for 2–3 minutes. Season with salt and pepper. Using the skimmer, transfer the stir-fry mixture to a platter. Bring the sauce to a simmer, add the cornflour mixture and simmer for about 1 minute until the sauce is thickened. Pour over the stir-fry mixture and serve over the rice.

TO DRINK:
A Californian Cabernet Sauvignon

[Serves 4]

450g skirt steak, halved lengthways and cut across the grain into 5mm slices

1 tablespoon finely chopped fresh ginger

2 tablespoons finely chopped garlic

½ bunch spring onions, white and green parts, cut 5mm thick

4 tablespoons oyster sauce

1 large head broccoli

ice cubes

5 tablespoons grapeseed or rapeseed oil

225g shiitake mushrooms, stems discarded and sliced 5mm thick

sea salt and freshly ground black pepper

225ml fresh chicken stock or stock make from a low-salt chicken stock cube

1 tablespoon cornflour mixed with 2 tablespoons water

–

50-50 Brown and White Rice, for serving (see page 12)

Ming's Tip:

If you don't enjoy the flavour of oysters, use vegetarian oyster sauce, now available from specialist suppliers and Asian food shops.

'French Dip' Orange Beef

This dish consists of orange-marinated beef rolls (or 'hoagies' as they are called in the USA), served with their cooking juices and stock, into which diners dip the sandwiches. Its forebear is Chicago's famous 'wet beef' sandwich, which is served 'au jus' – thus the title's 'French dip'. These are fun to make as well as eat, and are perfect for a hungry crowd. You might instruct diners to salute one another before they eat these with a 'here's looking at jus', but if you do, don't mention my name.

1. In a medium bowl, combine the orange juice, sambal, spring onion whites, ginger and shallots. Add the beef and stir to coat the slices. Cover and leave to marinate at room temperature for 15 minutes.

2. Drain the beef and reserve the marinade. Heat a wok over a high heat. Add 2 tablespoons of the oil and swirl to coat the pan. When the oil is hot, add half the beef and stir-fry for 4–5 minutes until cooked through. Transfer the beef to a plate. Add the remaining 2 tablespoons oil to the wok, swirl, stir-fry the remaining beef and transfer to the plate.

3. Add the stock and reserved marinade. Add the soy sauce if the stock is unsalted or low-salt. Add the orange zest and spring onion greens, season with salt and pepper and bring to the boil. Transfer the broth to four individual bowls.

4. Split the rolls in half. On the bottom halves place the tomato slices and top with the lettuce, then the beef. Cover with the roll tops and serve with the broth bowls for dipping the rolls into.

TO DRINK:
Yanjing beer from China

[Serves 4]

juice and grated zest of 2 oranges

1 tablespoon sambal or 1 finely chopped jalapeño chilli

1 bunch spring onions, thinly sliced, white and green parts separated

1 tablespoon finely chopped fresh ginger

2 shallots, thinly sliced

675g skirt steak, any silverskin removed, sliced as thinly as possible

4 tablespoons grapeseed or rapeseed oil

475ml fresh beef or chicken stock or stock made from a low-salt beef or chicken stock cube

1 tablespoon naturally brewed soy sauce, if needed

sea salt and freshly ground black pepper

–

4 long soft bread rolls

1 large tomato, sliced 5mm thick

1 small head iceberg lettuce, shredded

Ming's Tip:

To slice the beef easily, freeze it first for two hours. Rice crisps (see page 11) are the ideal accompaniment here.

green peppercorn beef with asparagus and rotini

Corkscrew-shaped rotini are awesome sauce-trappers, one reason I love them. Here, the pasta is paired with asparagus – a vegetable that gives its flavour-all when stir-fried – beef and green peppercorns. Steak with black peppercorns is a traditional match, but green peppercorns have a fresher yet pungent taste that goes beautifully with wok-cooked beef.

1. Fill a large bowl with water and add ice cubes. In a wok, cook the asparagus in abundant boiling salted water for 1–2 minutes until tender-crisp. Transfer to the iced water with a skimmer, and when cold, drain. Cut the asparagus into 5cm lengths and set aside.

2. Add more ice cubes to the bowl, if necessary. Return the water in the wok to the boil and cook the pasta for about 11 minutes until al dente. Transfer to the iced water, and when cold, drain and set aside.

3. Drain and dry the wok, then heat it over a high heat. Add 2 tablespoons of the oil and swirl to coat the bottom. When the oil is hot, add half the beef and stir-fry for 3–4 minutes until rare. Transfer to a plate. Add 2 more tablespoons of the oil, swirl, stir-fry the remaining beef and then transfer to the plate.

4. Add the remaining tablespoon of oil to the wok, swirl, and when the oil is hot, add the garlic, peppercorns and spring onions. Season with salt and pepper and stir-fry for about 2 minutes until soft. Return the beef to the wok, add the asparagus, pasta and stock and stir-fry for 3–4 minutes until heated through. Add the soy sauce and stir to blend. Adjust the seasoning, if necessary, and serve in four individual pasta dishes.

TO DRINK:
A spicy Shiraz, like Kangarilla Road Shiraz/Viognier from Australia

[Serves 4]

ice cubes

450g thin asparagus, ends trimmed

sea salt

225g dried rotini or fusilli pasta

5 tablespoons grapeseed or rapeseed oil

675g skirt steak, any silverskin removed, sliced on the bias 5mm thick

5 garlic cloves, thinly sliced

2 tablespoons crushed green peppercorns

1 bunch spring onions, white and green parts, thinly sliced

freshly ground black pepper

125ml fresh chicken stock or stock made from a low-salt chicken stock cube

2 tablespoons naturally brewed soy sauce

Ming's Tip:

To crush the peppercorns, arrange in a circle on a chopping board and crush with the back of a heavy pan.

TO DRINK:
Trimbach Riesling from Alsace,
France

[Serves 4]

2 tablespoons naturally brewed soy sauce

1 tablespoon finely chopped garlic

2 medium pork tenderloins (about 900g), any silverskin removed, cut into 5mm slices

225g mung bean noodles

3 tablespoons grapeseed or rapeseed oil

sea salt and freshly ground black pepper

1 medium red onion, halved lengthways and thinly sliced

400g cabbage kimchi

1 small courgette,
sliced as thinly as possible

225ml fresh chicken stock or stock made with a low-salt chicken stock cube

1/2 teaspoon Korean red chilli flakes or ancho chilli powder

pork kimchi with noodles

Stir-fried pork with kimchi is a beloved Korean dish. Kimchi, usually made from fermented cabbage, is wonderfully pungent – though I don't recommend playing spin-the-bottle after eating it. In addition to these ingredients, I've included satisfying mung bean noodles and courgettes. This is a terrific dish – real excitement on the plate.

1. In a medium bowl, combine the soy sauce and garlic. Add the pork and toss. Cover and leave to marinate in the refrigerator for 30 minutes.

2. Meanwhile, place the noodles in a wok and fill with hot water to cover. When the noodles have softened, after about 10 minutes, drain and transfer to a bowl.

3. Dry the wok and heat it over a high heat. Add 2 tablespoons of the oil and swirl to coat the pan. When the oil is hot, add the pork, season with salt and pepper and stir-fry for 6–8 minutes until just cooked through. Transfer the pork to a plate, add the remaining tablespoon of oil to the wok and swirl to coat the pan. When the oil is hot, add the onion and stir-fry for about 2 minutes until soft. Add the kimchi and courgette and season with salt and pepper. Add the pork, stock and the noodles, mix and heat through for 1–2 minutes.

4. Transfer to four individual serving bowls, garnish with the chilli flakes and serve immediately.

Ming's Tip:

A mandoline makes the job of slicing the courgettes, among other cutting chores, a breeze. If you don't own one, I suggest a ceramic model like the one Kyocera makes, which does the job quickly and is also inexpensive.

gingered pork with leeks

TO DRINK:
Chilled Mulderbosch Cabernet Sauvignon Rosé from South Africa

[Serves 4]

2 tablespoons organic Worcestershire sauce

1 tablespoon finely chopped garlic

1 tablespoon toasted sesame oil

2 serrano chillies, 1 finely chopped, 1 thinly sliced for garnish

2 tablespoons naturally brewed soy sauce

450g pork loin, very thinly sliced

3 tablespoons grapeseed or rapeseed oil

2 tablespoons peeled and finely sliced fresh ginger

3 large leeks, white parts, halved, cut into strips, washed and dried (see Ming's Tip)

sea salt and freshly ground black pepper

–

50-50 White and Brown Rice, for serving (see page 12)

Ming's Tip:

To cut the leeks into thin strips easily, halve the white parts length-ways and discard about one third of the interior. Flatten against your cutting surface and slice. Fill the bowl of a salad spinner with water, add the leeks and swish with your hands to remove any sand. Transfer the leeks to the spinner insert, throw out the water and rinse the bowl well. Spin the leeks dry.

I fell in love with leeks the first time I visited Paris. Wok-cooked, this wonderful member of the onion family has a bite and sweetness that other cooking methods don't deliver. Pork is a natural companion, as its subtle sweetness enhances that of the leeks – and vice versa. Heat from ginger and chilli helps to make this a completely winning dish.

1. In a medium bowl, combine the Worcestershire sauce, garlic, sesame oil, finely chopped chilli and soy sauce and mix together. Add the pork and stir gently to coat it. Cover and leave to marinate in the refrigerator for 30 minutes.

2. Drain the pork. Heat a wok over a high heat. Add 2 tablespoons of the oil and swirl to coat the pan. When the oil is hot, add the pork and stir-fry for 5–6 minutes until cooked through. Transfer the pork to a plate and set aside.

3. Add the remaining oil to the wok, swirl, and when the oil is hot, add the ginger. Stir-fry for 20 seconds, then add the leeks and season with salt and pepper. Stir-fry for about 2 minutes until the leeks are soft. Return the pork to the wok and heat through for 2–3 minutes.

4. Transfer to a serving bowl, garnish with the chilli slices and serve with the rice.

scallop and bacon fettuccine

I can eat scallops wrapped in bacon like peanuts. The combination of sweet and salty is perfect – and even better when paired with creamy fettuccine. As rich as all this might sound, I've made sure to keep the calories under control, and the dish non-cloying, by using yogurt in place of cream and adding spinach for its fresh green note.

1. Fill a large bowl with water and add ice cubes. In a wok, cook the fettuccine in abundant boiling salted water until al dente: about 3 minutes if fresh, 11 minutes if dry. Drain the pasta and transfer it to the iced water. When cold, drain the pasta and transfer it to a medium bowl. Coat the pasta lightly with oil and set it aside.

2. Line a plate with kitchen paper. Heat the wok over a medium heat. Add the bacon and stir-fry for 4–5 minutes until crisp. Using a skimmer, transfer the bacon to the plate.

3. Wipe out the wok and heat it over a medium-high heat. Add the 1 tablespoon oil and swirl to coat the pan. When the oil is hot, add the onions and ginger and stir-fry for about 3 minutes until soft. Add the scallops and stir-fry for 1 minute until almost cooked through. Add the wine and stock, deglaze the pan and simmer for 1–2 minutes to allow the liquid to reduce by one quarter. Add the yogurt, all but 1 tablespoon of the reserved bacon, the pasta, spinach and the chopped parsley. Toss gently to blend and heat through for about 2 minutes. Season with salt and pepper. Divide between four individual plates or pasta bowls, garnish with the parsley leaves and reserved bacon and serve.

TO DRINK:
An Italian rosé from Grignolino

[Serves 4]

ice cubes

225g fettuccine, fresh or dried

sea salt

1 tablespoon extra-virgin olive oil, plus more for coating the pasta

115g rashers streaky bacon, cut into 5mm pieces

1 medium red onion, cut into 5mm dice

1 tablespoon finely chopped fresh ginger

450g medium shelled scallops, cleaned and halved

125ml dry white wine

125ml fresh chicken stock or stock made from a low-salt chicken stock cube

125ml Greek yogurt

225g baby spinach leaves

2 tablespoons chopped fresh flat-leaf parsley, plus leaves for garnish

freshly ground black pepper

Ming's Tip:
You can make this with wholewheat fettuccine, which adds its own flavourful nuttiness.

TO DRINK:
An off-dry German Riesling

[Serves 4]

35g polenta

900g live clams

1 medium avocado, stoned, peeled and the flesh cut into 1cm dice (see Ming's Tip)

juice of I lime

sea salt and freshly ground black pepper

3 tablespoons grapeseed or rapeseed oil

225g lean pork mince

3 tablespoons finely chopped garlic

2 tablespoons finely chopped fresh ginger

1 bunch spring onions, white and green parts, cut into 2.5cm lengths (halve the white parts if large)

2 tablespoons sambal

2 tablespoons naturally brewed soy sauce

2 tablespoons naturally brewed rice vinegar

2 tablespoons honey

1 medium jicama, peeled and cut into 1cm dice

1 medium red pepper, deseeded and cut into 5mm dice (see Ming's Tip)

clams with pork and jicama

I based this dish on the great Portuguese favourite, *alentejana* – braised pork with clams. Wok cooking really brings out the best in this traditional pairing, which is enhanced by jicama and buttery avocado. I love translating a dish from one culture to another, which can really make the tried and true sing.

1. Fill a large bowl with water. Add the polenta, stir and add the clams. Leave the clams to purge for at least 1 hour and up to 3. Rinse, drain the clams well and set aside. Discard the water and polenta.

2. Meanwhile, place the avocado in a small bowl. Add the lime juice, season with salt and pepper and toss. Cover with clingfilm and set aside.

3. Heat a wok over a high heat. Add 1 tablespoon of the oil and swirl to coat the pan. When the oil is hot, add the pork, season with salt and pepper and stir-fry, breaking up the pork, for 6–8 minutes until brown. Transfer the pork to a plate.

4. Add the remaining 2 tablespoons of the oil to the wok and swirl to coat. Add the clams and stir-fry for about 4 minutes until they start to open. Add the garlic, ginger, spring onions, sambal, soy sauce, vinegar and honey. Return the pork to the wok, add the jicama and red pepper, cover and cook for about 4 minutes until the clams open fully. Discard any clams that haven't opened.

5. Transfer the stir-fry to a platter, sprinkle with the avocado and serve.

Ming's Tip:

To dice an avocado, halve it lengthways, remove the stone and separate the flesh from the peel. Slice the flesh parallel to your cutting surface, cut the stacked slices lengthways, then cut crossways to dice. To dice a pepper easily, first cut away both ends. Cut downwards into the pepper on one long side and 'peel' away its flesh by rolling the pepper while you cut. You'll have separated the useable part of the pepper from its core and seeds. Halve the useable part and stack the halves. Slice lengthways, then cut crossways to dice.

black bean scallops and courgettes

In China, scallops with black beans is second in popularity to black beans and clams. For my money, the first combo is the best, as the scallops' sweetness makes a perfect foil for the beans' salty savour. This easy dish also features courgettes, an underused vegetable that has great colour and texture and is also inexpensive. It's made quickly too.

1. Heat a wok over a medium-high heat. Add the oil and swirl to coat the bottom. When the oil is hot, add the black beans, garlic and spring onion whites. Season with salt and pepper and sauté for about 1 minute until softened. Add the scallops and courgettes and sauté for 5–6 minutes until the scallops are just cooked through.

2. Add the butter and adjust the seasoning, if necessary. Add the spring onion greens and stir to combine.

3. Transfer the stir-fry to four individual serving plates and serve with the rice on the side.

TO DRINK:
Yanjing beer from China

[Serves 4]

2 tablespoons grapeseed or rapeseed oil

2 tablespoons finely chopped fermented black beans

1 tablespoon finely chopped garlic

1 bunch spring onions, thinly sliced, white and green parts separated

sea salt and freshly ground black pepper

450g medium shelled scallops, cleaned and halved

250g trimmed courgettes, sliced 5mm thick

25g unsalted butter

–

50-50 White and Brown Rice, for serving (see page 12)

black pepper sake mussels with granny smith apples

TO DRINK:
An Alsatian Riesling like Trimbach

Apples may seem an odd mate for mussels, but the pairing is inspired, if I say so myself. The apples' tart-sweetness plays beautifully against the sweetness of the mussels – and sake, which can have a faint apple nuance, furthers the flavour play. Black pepper, generously included, adds resonance. This is another quick dish.

1. Heat a wok over a high heat. Add the oil and swirl to coat the pan. When the oil is hot, add the garlic, shallots and coarse black pepper and stir-fry for 30 seconds. Add the mussels and season with salt and pepper. Add the sake, deglaze the pan and cover. When the mussels have begun to open, after about 3 minutes, add the apples and butter. (Discard any mussels that haven't opened.)

2. Continue to cook for about 2 minutes until the flavours have combined. Adjust the seasoning, if necessary. Transfer to a large serving bowl, sprinkle with the togarashi and serve.

[Serves 4]

2 tablespoons grapeseed or rapeseed oil

1 tablespoon finely chopped garlic

3 large shallots, thinly sliced

1 tablespoon coarsely ground black pepper

900g live mussels, cleaned and debearded

sea salt and freshly ground black pepper

125ml sake

2 Granny Smith apples, unpeeled, cored and cut into fine strips

55g unsalted butter

pinches of togarashi or other hot pepper, for garnish

mirin clams and leeks

Although we've done a very successful version of this dish at Blue Ginger, I keep reinventing it. I get very involved with flavour matching – especially with the way mirin's sweetness complements that of leeks so beautifully and how both do wonders for clams. This time around I've added bacon and, I think, created a winner.

1. Fill a large bowl with water. Add the polenta, stir and add the clams. Leave the clams to purge for at least 1 hour and up to 3. Rinse, drain the clams well and set aside. Discard the water and polenta.

2. Heat a wok over a medium-high heat. Add the oil and swirl to coat the pan. When the oil is hot, add the bacon and stir-fry for about 3 minutes until crisp. Pour off all but 1 tablespoon of the fat. Add the clams and stir-fry for about 2 minutes until they start to open.

3. Add the garlic, jalapeño and leeks and stir-fry for about 3 minutes until softened. Season with salt and pepper. Add the mirin, deglaze the pan, cover and cook for 4–6 minutes until all the clams have opened. Discard any clams that remain unopened. Add the yogurt and lemon juice and stir. Transfer to a platter or four large serving bowls and serve.

TO DRINK:
A Chenin Blanc, like Spier Discover Steen from South Africa

[Serves 4]

35g polenta

900g live clams or cockles

1 tablespoon grapeseed or rapeseed oil

2 rashers back bacon, finely diced

4 garlic cloves, thinly sliced

1 large jalapeño chilli, preferably red, unseeded and thinly sliced

2 large leeks, white parts, halved, cut into very thin strips, washed and dried (see Ming's Tip, page 47)

sea salt and freshly ground black pepper

175ml mirin

4 tablespoons Greek yogurt

juice of 1 lemon

Ming's Tip:
This dish really requires crusty bread for sopping, as no one will want to miss a bit of the sauce.

tamari tofu stir-fry
with rice noodles

TO DRINK:
Robert Mondavi Riesling

I love rice noodles in all their forms. This dish features rice vermicelli, which are long and thin and have a wonderfully chewy texture. Tofu, the dish's centrepiece, receives ample flavouring from the tamari, which also enhances the broccoli's sweetness – and hot sauce adds its kick. Tofu sceptics will be instantly won over by this delectable dish.

1. In a medium bowl, combine the tamari, hot sauce, garlic and ginger. Add the tofu and stir gently. Cover and leave to marinate for 15 minutes.

2. Meanwhile, fill a large bowl with water and add ice cubes. Bring abundant salted water to the boil in a wok. Add the broccoli, blanch for 30 seconds, and using a large sieve, transfer the broccoli to the iced water. When the broccoli is cold, drain and set aside. Don't drain the wok water.

3. Add more ice cubes to the bowl, if necessary. Add 475ml cold water to the wok. Add the noodles and leave for about 10 minutes to soften. Using the sieve, transfer the noodles to the iced water, and when cold, drain and set aside.

4. Drain the water from the wok and dry it. Heat it over a high heat, add the oil and swirl to coat the pan. When the oil is hot, add the spring onion whites and stir-fry for about 30 seconds until soft. Add the tofu with its marinade and stir-fry for about 2 mintues until heated through. Return the broccoli and noodles to the wok, toss gently to combine and heat through for about 2 minutes. Season with salt and pepper.

5. Transfer the stir-fry to a four individual serving bowls, garnish with the spring onion greens and serve with the lemon wedges, if you like, for squeezing over the dish.

[Serves 4]

4 tablespoons wheat-free tamari sauce

1–2 tablespoons hot sauce

1 tablespoon finely chopped garlic

1 tablespoon finely chopped fresh ginger

ice cubes

one 400g pack firm tofu, cut into 1cm dice

sea salt

1 head broccoli, florets separated, stems peeled, squared and cut into thin strips

225g rice vermicelli

2 tablespoons grapeseed or rapeseed oil

1 bunch spring onions, thinly sliced, white and green parts separated

freshly ground black pepper

1 lemon, cut into wedges (optional)

cauliflower and shiitake mushroom stir-fry

TO DRINK:
A French rosé, like Couly-Dutheil René Chinon

[Serves 4]

ice cubes

sea salt

1 small head cauliflower, separated into florets

25g unsalted butter

60g panko (Japanese breadcrumbs)

2 tablespoons grapeseed or rapeseed oil

2 tablespoons finely chopped garlic

1 tablespoon finely chopped fresh ginger

125g shiitake caps, quartered if large, halved if medium

4 tablespoons vegetarian oyster sauce

grated zest and juice of 1 lemon

freshly ground black pepper

50-50 White and Brown Rice, for serving (see page 12)

1 tablespoon finely sliced chives, for garnish

In this simple stir-fry, the mushroom flavour comes through loud and clear. Cauliflower has something of a dubious rep due to indifferent preparation, but in this dish it's subtly delicious.

1. Fill a large bowl with water and ice cubes. Bring abundant salted water to the boil in a wok. Add the cauliflower and blanch for 30 seconds, drain and transfer it to the iced water. When the cauliflower is cold, drain it, transfer it to a plate and set aside.

2. Dry the wok, add the butter and heat over a high heat. When it has melted, add the panko and stir-fry gently for about 1 minute until the panko is golden brown – watch carefully to avoid burning. Transfer the panko to a medium bowl.

3. Wipe out the wok and heat over a high heat. Add the oil and swirl to coat the pan. When the oil is hot, add the garlic, ginger and mushrooms and stir-fry for about 2 minutes until softened. Add the cauliflower, oyster sauce and lemon zest and juice. Season with salt and pepper and cook, stirring, for 2–3 minutes to heat through.

4. Make a bed of the rice on a platter, or transfer to four individual serving bowls, and top with the stir-fry. Sprinkle with the panko, garnish with the chives and serve.

3

Traditional sautéing involves searing ingredients in an oil-coated frying pan. These are tossed or stirred as they brown. I applaud the tried and true, but why limit sautéing to one shallow utensil? My one-pot method introduces pot sautéing – searing in a tall, wide pan into which other ingredients are then added to create a delicious 'meal in one'. Dishes such as Black Bean Orecchiette with Spicy Pork and Broccoli and Seared Curried Cod with Warm Olive Chutney are based on this easy, innovative – and spatter-free – approach.

I also take advantage of traditional sautéing to create exciting recastings of old favourites – like Asian Sloppy Joes – as well as other 'innovations', such as Potato-Crusted Halibut with Shaved Fennel Salad, and Loin Lamb Chops with Augergine and Lemongrass Tzatziki. Sautéing has never been considered a particularly versatile method, but by following my one-pot approach, it is.

SAUTÉ

chicken meatballs with penne and tomato sauce

Everyone loves meatballs and pasta. The meatballs in this dish are made with chicken, which is every bit as good as the beef-based kind, not to mention better for you; penne, the quill-shaped pasta, has great mouthfeel and traps sauce beautifully. Because chicken is a lean meat, I add panko – Japanese breadcrumbs – to the meatball mixture so that everything coheres. And to make this dish especially easy, I call for shop-bought tomato sauce as a base for the pasta accompaniment. Get your favourite brand and you're in business.

1. Fill a large bowl with water and add ice cubes. In a tall, wide saucepan, cook the pasta in abundant salted boiling water for about 11 minutes until al dente. Using a large sieve, drain the pasta and transfer in the sieve to the iced water. When the pasta is cold, drain and transfer to a medium bowl. Drizzle in enough oil to coat it lightly and toss. Set aside.

2. Heat the pan over a medium-high heat. Add 2 tablespoons of the oil and swirl to coat the bottom. When the oil is hot, add the onions and garlic and sauté for about 6 minutes until browned. Transfer to a large bowl. Reserve the pan.

3. When the onion mixture is cool, add the panko, chicken and eggs. Season with salt and pepper. Blend lightly and test the seasoning by sautéing or microwaving a bit of it. Adjust the seasoning, if necessary. With wet hands, form the mixture into meatballs the size of ping-pong balls.

4. Heat the pan over a high heat. Add the remaining 2 tablespoons of oil and swirl to coat the bottom. When the oil is hot and working in batches, if necessary, add the meatballs. Sauté the meatballs on all sides for 4–5 minutes until browned. Add the spring onions, tomato sauce and basil, reduce the heat to medium-low and simmer for about 10 minutes to blend the flavours. Add the pasta and mix well. Season with salt and pepper and serve.

TO DRINK:
A good Italian country red, like Altesino Rosso di Moutalcino

[Serves 4]

ice cubes

450g dried penne

sea salt

4 tablespoons extra-virgin olive oil, plus extra for coating the pasta

1 large onion, finely chopped

1 tablespoon finely chopped garlic

30g panko (Japanese breadcrumbs)

450g chicken mince

2 large eggs

freshly ground black pepper

1 bunch spring onions, white and green parts, thinly sliced

2 x 500g jars best-quality shop-bought tomato pasta sauce

20 Thai basil leaves or regular basil leaves

loin lamb chops with aubergine and lemongrass tzatziki

The Greeks may not have been the first to pair lamb and yogurt, but they've done a bang-up job with the match. Tzatziki is the delicious yogurt medium that, in my rendering, includes lemongrass. The chops are served on aubergine slices, which sop up their delicious juice. This is a perfect summertime dish, great for outdoor barbecuing; but it's equally satisfying year round.

1. Peel the cucumber and quarter it lengthways. Place it in a colander, sprinkle generously with salt and leave to drain for 30 minutes. Rinse the cucumber and cut into 5mm dice.

2. Meanwhile, peel the aubergine lengthways into 1cm strips 'zebra-style', leaving a 1cm strip of skin between each peel. Cut the aubergine widthways into eight 2.5cm slices. Set aside.

3. To make the tzatziki, heat a large sauté pan over a high heat. Add 1 tablespoon of the oil and swirl to coat the bottom. When the oil is hot, add the lemongrass and garlic and sauté, stirring, for about 3 minutes until soft. Don't allow the mixture to colour. Transfer to a small bowl, and when cool, add the yogurt, cucumber, mint and lemon juice. Mix well and season with salt and pepper, then cover and refrigerate.

4. Season the lamb chops with salt and pepper. Heat the pan over a medium-high heat. Add the remaining 2 tablespoons of oil and swirl to coat the bottom. When the oil is hot, add the lamb chops and sauté for about 10 minutes until browned on both sides. Transfer to a plate and set aside.

5. Meanwhile, brush the aubergine on both sides with oil and season with salt and pepper. Working in batches, add the aubergine to the pan and sauté, turning once, for 4–6 minutes until the slices are lightly coloured. Arrange the aubergine on a platter and top each slice with a chop. Serve with the tzatziki on the side.

TO DRINK:
A Cabernet Sauvignon, like Honig from California

[Serves 4]

1 small cucumber

sea salt

1 aubergine

3 tablespoons extra-virgin olive oil, plus more for the aubergine

2 tablespoons finely chopped lemongrass, light part only (see Ming's Tip)

3 tablespoons finely chopped garlic

225ml Greek yogurt

8 mint leaves, cut into 3mm strips

juice and grated zest of 1 lemon

freshly ground black pepper

8 loin lamb chops (about 1.3kg)

Ming's Tip:

To finely chop lemongrass, hit the light part with the side of a knife several times to break it down. The root end should pop off; if not, cut it away. Starting where the light part joins the darker, slice the light part lengthways three or four times. Cut the light part crossways and then finely chop. (You can use the darker part to make stock.)

asian spaghetti

TO DRINK:
A Dolcetto d'Alba, like Prunotto

[Serves 4]

ice cubes

450g dried spaghetti

sea salt

1 tablespoon extra-virgin olive oil, plus more for coating the pasta

2 large onions, cut into 5mm dice

2 tablespoons finely chopped garlic

450g lean beef mince

450g lean pork mince

freshly ground black pepper

900g canned whole Italian plum tomatoes with their juice

4 tablespoons naturally brewed soy sauce

2 tablespoons tomato purée

15g Thai basil

Close your eyes, envision a spaghetti dish and I bet you see tomato sauce. My attempt to transform the typical spaghetti-ragù pairing inspired this dish, which does include tomatoes but is otherwise exceptional. The key here is the addition of soy sauce, which adds *umami*, that intriguing 'fifth taste' first explored by Japanese cooks. It also features Thai basil, one of my favourite herbs. This is much loved in my house and should be equally welcome in yours.

1. Fill a large bowl with water and add ice cubes. In a large saucepan, cook the pasta in abundant boiling salted water for about 11 minutes until al dente. Drain and add to the iced water. When the pasta is cold, drain, coat lightly with oil and set aside.

2. Heat the pan over a medium-high heat. Add the 1 tablespoon oil, and when hot, add the onions and garlic. Sauté, stirring, for about 2 minutes until the onions are translucent. Add the beef and pork, season with salt and pepper and sauté, stirring to break up the meat, for about 5 minutes until lightly browned. Add the tomatoes with their juice, the soy sauce, tomato purée and basil and bring to a simmer. Adjust the seasoning, if necessary, and simmer for about 25 minutes until the liquid is reduced by a quarter. Add the reserved pasta to the pan and stir gently. Transfer to a platter or four individual plates and serve.

TO DRINK:
A pilsner lager, like Stella Artois

[Serves 4]

2 tablespoons grapeseed or rapeseed oil

2 medium red onions, cut into 5mm dice

2 tablespoons finely chopped garlic

1 tablespoon finely chopped fresh ginger

100g celery, diced

1 tablespoon sambal or hot sauce of your choice

300ml hoisin sauce

450g lean beef mince

450g lean pork mince

juice of 2 limes

225g plum tomatoes, fresh or canned, chopped

sea salt and freshly ground black pepper

4 hamburger buns

1 small head iceberg lettuce, shredded

–

rice crisps

pickles, for serving

asian sloppy joes

Sloppy Joes were my mum's go-to dish when famished kids hung out at my house growing up. Of course, she gave it her own Asian twist, which I honour here: hoisin sauce for a touch of sweetness, ginger, pork, plus beef, garlic – of course – and a bit of sambal for heat. Adults are equally delighted by this easy, informal dish, which always looks invitingly, well, sloppy. Rice crisps are the indispensible accompaniment here.

1. Heat a tall, wide saucepan over a high heat. Add the oil and swirl to coat the bottom. When the oil is hot, add the onions, garlic, ginger, celery and sambal. Sauté, stirring occasionally, for about 2 minutes until the onions are soft. Add the hoisin sauce and sauté for 1 minute. Add the beef and pork and sauté, breaking up the meat, for about 6 minutes until just cooked through. Add the lime juice and tomatoes and season with salt and pepper. Reduce the heat to medium-low and simmer for 20–25 minutes until the mixture has thickened enough to mound when ladled.

2. Toast the buns and place a bottom half on each individual serving plate. Top generously with the meat mixture. Top with the lettuce and the bun tops. Serve with rice crisps and pickles.

Ming's Tip:
Make extra sloppy joe mixture, transfer to freezer bags and freeze. It's great to have on hand for quick meal making.

black bean orecchiette with spicy pork and broccoli

I'm a huge orecchiette fan. The 'tiny ears' are exceptionally chewy and really hold other ingredients, like the spicy pork in this recipe. The pork is complemented by fermented black beans, one of the deep Chinese flavourings; I think of them as soy sauce on steroids. This is a terrifically tasty dish and one, I've found, that kids really love. Serve it with big soup spoons and everyone's happy.

1. Separate the broccoli into florets. Cut off their long stems and, using a chef's knife, square the stems so that they resemble elongated blocks. Alternatively, peel the stems. Cut the stems into 5mm pieces.

2. Fill a bowl large bowl with water and add ice cubes. Bring abundant salted water to the boil in a tall, wide saucepan. Add the broccoli and blanch for 30 seconds, retrieve the broccoli with a large sieve and transfer it in the sieve to the iced water. When the broccoli is cold, lift the sieve and drain the broccoli. Transfer the broccoli to a plate.

3. Return the water in the pan to the boil. Add more ice cubes to the bowl, if needed. Add the pasta to the pan and cook for about 10 minutes until al dente. Retrieve the pasta with the sieve and transfer to the bowl. Reserve 125ml of the cooking water. When the pasta is cold, lift the sieve and drain the pasta.

4. Dry the pan and heat over a medium heat. Add the olive oil to the pan and swirl to coat the bottom. When the oil is hot, add the garlic, black beans, ginger and onions and sauté, stirring, for about 2 minutes until the onions are soft. Add the wine, deglaze the pan and simmer for about 2 minutes until the liquid is reduced by half. Season with salt and pepper. Add the pork and sauté, breaking up the meat, for 6–8 minutes until just cooked through.

5. Add the pasta and broccoli to the black-bean mixture and toss well. If the mixture seems dry, add the reserved cooking water. Season again with salt and pepper. Transfer to a large serving bowl or platter, garnish with the chilli flakes, drizzle with olive oil and serve.

TO DRINK:
A crisp Pinot Grigio, like Maso Canali from Italy

[Serves 4]

1 large head broccoli

ice cubes

sea salt

225g dried orecchiette

2 tablespoons extra-virgin olive oil, plus more for drizzling

1 tablespoon finely chopped garlic

2 tablespoons fermented black beans

1 tablespoon finely chopped fresh ginger

1 medium red onion, cut into 5mm dice

225ml dry white wine

freshly ground black pepper

450g lean pork mince

1 teaspoon Korean red chilli flakes or other red chilli flakes, for garnish

soba noodle carbonara

TO DRINK:
A light fruity Italian white wine, like Friulano de Friuli

[Serves 4]

ice cubes

115g soba noodles

sea salt

1 tablespoon grapeseed or rapeseed oil

85g pancetta, cut into 5mm dice

5 spring onions, thinly sliced, white and green parts separated

1 tablespoon finely chopped garlic

125ml double cream

about 25g Parmigiano-Reggiano cheese, freshly grated, plus more for serving

3 tablespoons pasteurized liquid egg yolks or beaten fresh egg yolks

freshly ground black pepper

Trying to make a good dish even better is a challenge I love. In the case of spaghetti carbonara, that much-enjoyed Italian speciality featuring pancetta, eggs and cheese, my first move was to substitute soba noodles for the spaghetti. Not only is buckwheat-based soba better for you than regular pasta, but it packs more flavour. Spring onions, courtesy of the Asian storecupboard, add their own kick.

1. Fill a large bowl with water and add ice cubes. In a tall saucepan, cook the soba in abundant boiling salted water for 3–4 minutes until al dente. Drain the noodles, reserving 75ml of the cooking water, using a large sieve and transfer to the iced water. When the noodles are cold, drain and set aside.

2. Heat the pan over a medium-high heat. Add the oil and swirl to coat the bottom. When the oil is hot, add the pancetta. Sauté, stirring, for 6–8 minutes until crisp. Add the spring onion whites and garlic and sauté for 1 minute. Add the cream, the reserved cooking water and the cheese. Add the soba and toss to combine. Add the eggs and toss gently. Season with salt and pepper. Transfer immediately to four individual plates, garnish with the spring onion greens and serve with additional cheese.

Ming's Tip:

As the egg yolks remain uncooked in this, I call for pasteurized liquid yolks to ensure safety, but you can use fresh egg yolks if you prefer.

TO DRINK:
A French Burgundy, like Louis Latour Santenay

[Serves 4]

2 tablespoons grapeseed or rapeseed oil

450g small, uncooked peeled prawns, rinsed and dried

sea salt and freshly ground black pepper

35g unsalted butter

2 tablespoons finely chopped garlic

1 small onion, cut into 3mm dice

370g koshikari or other sushi rice, or Arborio rice

225ml dry white wine

1.2–1.4 litres fresh chicken stock or stock-made from low-salt chicken stock cubes, hot

12 Thai basil leaves, cut into very fine strips

juice of 1 lime

thai basil prawn risotto

Some people think risotto is tricky to make. It's not. All you have to do is pay attention as you add ladlefuls of stock to the rice so that you can judge when the risotto is properly cooked. My Asian version features koshikari rice, a premium sushi rice that has a higher absorption threshold than that of other rices. Like its Italian cousin Arborio, it can be cooked to a creamy-firm bite. Prawns and Thai basil complete the dish.

1. Heat a large saucepan over a medium-high heat. Add 1 tablespoon of the oil and swirl to coat the bottom. When the oil is hot, add the prawns and sauté, stirring, for about 1 minute until pink. Season with salt and pepper. Transfer the prawns to a plate and set aside.

2. Add the remaining tablespoon of oil and 15g of the butter. When the mixture is hot, add the garlic and onions and sauté for 1–2 minutes until soft. Add the rice and sauté, stirring, for about 2 minutes until the rice has become opaque. Add the wine, deglaze the pan and simmer for 2–3 minutes until the liquid has been absorbed by the rice.

3. Ladle in the stock 125ml at a time, allowing each addition to be absorbed by the rice before adding the next. Continue for about 10 minutes until the rice is al dente. Return the prawns to the rice, add the basil, remaining 20g butter and the lime juice and stir. Taste and adjust the seasoning.

4. Transfer the risotto to four individual serving bowls and serve.

mum's famous vinegared prawns

It's true: I have the world's best mum. She also makes the world's best food, including the traditional version of this prawn dish, a beloved favourite of my childhood. It's based on a Chinese seasoning combination called 3-2-1, the proportion of sugar to soy sauce to vinegar in the recipe. Here, I use two vinegars – balsamic for its dark sweetness, rice vinegar for tartness – plus edamame, for texture. I also 'francophile' the dish with butter, a touch that adds lusciousness. And there's potatoes – another departure from Mum's dish, but delicious even so.

1. Preheat the oven to 190°C/375°F/Gas Mark 5.

2. Wrap the potatoes in foil, prick them several times with a fork and bake for about 30 minutes until cooked through.

3. Meanwhile, in a medium bowl combine the vinegars, sugar and soy sauce and stir until the sugar is dissolved. Set aside.

4. Heat a large sauté pan over a high heat. Add 1 tablespoon of the oil. Add the prawns and sauté, stirring, for about 1 minute until the prawns turn pink. Transfer to a bowl and set aside.

5. Add the remaining oil to the pan, and when hot, add the garlic, ginger and shallots. Sauté for about 2 minutes until soft. Add the soy sauce mixture, deglaze the pan and simmer for 2–3 minutes until the mixture is reduced by half. Add the edamame, tomato and prawns. Simmer for 2–3 minutes until the prawns are cooked through. Whisk in the butter and season with salt and pepper.

6. Trim the ends from the potatoes and halve through the centre. Divide the potatoes between four individual plates, top with the prawns and sauce and then serve.

TO DRINK:
A white Burgundy, like Latour Puligny Montrachet or any other Montrachet

[Serves 4]

4 Yukon Gold or Estima potatoes, each about 7.5cm in diameter

4 tablespoons balsamic vinegar

4 tablespoons naturally brewed rice vinegar

1 tablespoon sugar

1 tablespoon plus 1 teaspoon naturally brewed soy sauce

2 tablespoons grapeseed or rapeseed oil

12 large uncooked prawns, peeled and deveined

2 tablespoons finely chopped garlic

1 tablespoon finely chopped fresh ginger

2 medium shallots, thinly sliced

150g shelled edamame

1 medium tomato, cut into 5mm dice

55g chilled unsalted butter

sea salt and freshly ground black pepper

TO DRINK:
A tropical fruit juice, like pineapple or passion fruit, or a New Zealand Sauvignon Blanc, like Brancott or Giesen

[Serves 4]

ice cubes

225g fresh or dried pappardelle

sea salt

2 tablespoons extra-virgin olive oil, plus more for coating the pasta

2 tablespoons finely chopped lemongrass, white part only (see Ming's Tip, page 66)

4 shallots, thinly sliced

1 tablespoon finely chopped garlic

freshly ground black pepper

12 large uncooked prawns, peeled and deveined

grated zest and juice of 2 lemons

35g unsalted butter

1 tablespoon thinly sliced chives, for garnish

lemongrass scampi with pappardelle

The Italian-American dish called 'shrimp scampi' (a redundancy, since 'scampi' is always a prawn dish) features prawns, garlic butter, lemon and parsley. We've had much success at Blue Ginger serving this version with lemongrass in addition to the citrus fruit, and pairing the prawns with pappardelle, a pasta with lots of surface area for sauce-coating. This is a perfect starter or main dish, and it's easy to make too.

1. Fill a large bowl with water and add ice cubes. In a tall, wide saucepan, cook the pappardelle in abundant boiling salted water until al dente: 1–2 minutes if fresh, 4–5 minutes if dried. Using a large sieve, transfer the pasta to the iced water, and when cold, drain and transfer to a medium bowl. Drizzle in enough oil to coat the pasta lightly, toss and set aside. Reserve 225ml of the cooking water.

2. Heat the pan over a medium heat. Add the 2 tablespoons oil and swirl to coat the bottom. When the oil is hot, add the lemongrass, shallots and garlic and sauté, stirring, for 1 minute. Season with salt and pepper. Add the prawns and sauté for 3–5 minutes until cooked through. Add the lemon zest and juice, stir and return the pasta to the pan. Toss to combine. Adjust the seasoning, if necessary. If the mixture seems dry, add as much of the reserved pasta water, starting with 2 tablespoons, as needed. Add the butter, stir and transfer to four individual serving plates. Garnish with the chives and serve.

seared curried cod
with warm olive chutney

A curry rub not only gives the fish a great flavour, but helps to colour it richly. I devised this dish after tasting South African cooking, which melds native and European ingredients intriguingly – my inspiration for putting olives in the sprightly chutney accompaniment. Curry and olives is one of those great combos that people should be more aware of, and definitely will be when they try this.

1. On a large platter, combine the curry powder and rice flour and mix well. Season the fish with salt and pepper and then dredge on both sides in the flour mixture.

2. Heat a large, heavy frying pan that can be brought to the table over a medium-high heat. When the pan is very hot, add 2 tablespoons of the oil and swirl to coat the bottom. When the oil is hot, add the fish. Sauté the fish, turning once, for about 8 minutes until a paring knife pierces it easily. Remove the fish from the pan and set aside.

3. Add the remaining 2 tablespoons of oil, swirl, and when hot, add the shallots, olives, tomato and orange juice. Heat through for about 2 minutes. Add the coriander and stir to combine.

4. Return the fish to the pan, drizzle with oil and serve.

TO DRINK:
A Chenin Blanc, like Domaine Vigneau-Chevreau Cuvée Silex Vouvray from France

[Serves 4]

4 tablespoons Madras curry powder

80g white or brown rice flour, or cornflour

four 175–225g cod fillets

sea salt and freshly ground black pepper

4 tablespoons extra-virgin olive oil, plus more for drizzling

3 shallots, finely chopped

80g mixed olives, pitted and finely chopped

1 large tomato, cut into 5mm dice

juice of 1 orange

2 tablespoons chopped fresh coriander

Ming's Tip:

To prevent the fish from sticking to the pan, make sure the pan is very hot before adding oil. The oil should appear to shimmer or dance before adding the fish. If the fish sticks anyway, don't try to dislodge it. Allow the fish to crust and it will release by itself.

soba noodle prawn pancakes

This is my take on Japanese *okonomiyaki*, pancakes with savoury toppings. In some okonomiyaki restaurants, customers cook their own pancakes on an iron griddle set in the table. My kitchen-cooked version uses soba noodles to make free-form pancake 'sandwiches', which are filled with a delicious, prawn-based purée. These are fun to do, and they make an impressive showing for guests.

1. Fill a large bowl with water and add ice cubes. In a large saucepan, cook the noodles in abundant boiling salted water for about 5 minutes until al dente. Using a large sieve, drain and transfer the noodles to the iced water. When the noodles are cold, drain and set aside.

2. Heat the pan over a medium heat. Add the pancetta and sauté for 8–10 minutes until crisp. Drain the pancetta on kitchen paper and set aside.

3. In a small bowl, combine the mayonnaise, Worcestershire sauce and the larger quantity of spring onion greens. Season with salt and pepper. Set aside.

4. Add the eggs and prawns to a food processor and pulse until the mixture is roughly puréed. Transfer the mixture to a medium bowl, add the parsley, pancetta and spring onion whites and fold to combine.

5. To make the pancakes, divide the noodles into 16 equal portions and place on a work surface. Flatten to make 16 pancakes about 7.5cm in diameter. Top each with 1 heaped tablespoon of the prawn purée, top with the remaining noodles and flatten to make 1cm-thick pancakes.

6. Add the oil to a non-stick sauté pan and heat over a medium-high heat. Using a spatula, and working in batches if necessary, add the pancakes and sauté, turning once, for 4–5 minutes until crispy.

7. Place streaks of the mayonnaise mixture on serving plates, top with the pancakes, garnish with the remaining spring onion greens and serve.

TO DRINK:
A Californian Marsanne

[Serves 4]

ice cubes

225g soba noodles

sea salt

85g pancetta, cut into 1cm dice

115g mayonnaise

1 tablespoon organic Worcestershire sauce

1 bunch spring onions, thinly sliced, white and green parts separated, 1 tablespoon greens reserved for garnish

freshly ground black pepper

2 large eggs

450g small, uncooked peeled prawns, rinsed and drained

4 tablespoons chopped flat-leaf parsley

2 tablespoons grapeseed or rapeseed oil, plus more, if needed

TO DRINK:
A chilled sake

[Serves 4]

juice of 2 limes

6 tablespoons grapeseed or rapeseed oil

2 tablespoons chopped chives

3 fennel bulbs, cored and very thinly sliced (see Ming's Tip, page 45)

sea salt and freshly ground black pepper

2 eggs

160g white rice flour or plain flour

60g dehydrated mashed potato flakes

450g skinless halibut, cut into four 115g fillets

potato-crusted halibut with shaved fennel salad

This is one of my favourite springtime-summertime dishes. Halibut, a lean, mild-tasting fish, is coated with rice flour and dehydrated potato flakes – a terrific, more delicate alternative to breadcrumbs – sautéed and served with a lime-dressed fennel salad. You'll be amazed at the tasty elegance of this dish, which is really fun to do too.

1. To make the salad, combine the lime juice, 4 tablespoons of the oil and the chives in a large bowl and whisk to blend. Just before cooking the fish, add the fennel to the bowl, stir, season with salt and pepper and leave to macerate while the fish cooks.

2. Beat the eggs lightly in a shallow bowl. Spread the flour on a medium plate and the potato flakes on a second. Season the fish with salt and pepper on both sides. One by one, coat the fish fillets lightly with the flour, dip them into the egg and then coat with the potato flakes.

3. Heat a large sauté pan over a medium heat. Add the remaining 2 tablespoons of oil and swirl to coat the bottom. When the oil is hot, add the fish and sauté, turning once, for about 6 minutes until the fish is golden brown and just cooked through. Divide the salad between four individual serving plates, top with the fish and serve.

vegetarian paella

To me, paella is the best family-style dish ever. The traditional version is, however, something of a production, involving multiple kinds of seafood plus, usually, chicken and sausage. My take uses vegetables only, including sweet potato and edamame, and sushi rice, which absorbs more of the flavourful braising liquid than other types. The dish is rich and satisfying, so you never miss the seafood.

1. Heat a large paella pan or large frying pan over a medium-high heat. Add the oil and swirl to coat the bottom. When the oil is hot, add the onions, lemongrass, garlic and ginger and sauté, stirring, for about 2 minutes until soft. Season with salt and pepper.

2. Add the rice and paprika and sauté, stirring, until the rice is coated with oil. Add the wine, deglaze the pan and simmer for about 2 minutes until the liquid is reduced by three quarters. Add the stock and parsley, stir and add the potato and edamame. Adjust the seasoning, if necessary. Reduce the heat to low and simmer gently, covered, for 25–30 minutes until the rice is cooked. Leave to rest for 5 minutes and serve from the pan.

TO DRINK:
A Spanish rosé, like Muga Rioja

[Serves 4]

2 tablespoons extra-virgin olive oil

1 large onion, finey chopped

4 lemongrass stalks, white part only, finely chopped (see Ming's Tip, page 66)

2 tablespoons finely chopped garlic

1 tablespoon finely chopped fresh ginger

sea salt and freshly ground black pepper

370g sushi rice

1 tablespoon paprika

225ml dry white wine

950ml vegetable stock

½ bunch flat-leaf parsley, roughly chopped

1 large sweet potato, cut into 1cm dice

150g shelled edamame

asian ratatouille with wholemeal couscous

If you doubt that a meatless dish can be just as satisfying as one that isn't, you must try this. I first made ratatouille in Paris – a bit far from its terroir, but a revelation to me nonetheless. Prepared with the super-flavourful fermented black beans and other Asian ingredients, and served with wholemeal couscous, ratatouille becomes a really mighty dish, and one that's surprisingly light.

1. Heat a medium sauté pan over a high heat. Add 2 tablespoons of the oil, and when hot, add the onions and aubergine. Season with salt and pepper and sauté, stirring, for about 3 minutes until the vegetables are soft. Add the garlic and beans and sauté for 1 minute. Add the red peppers and courgettes and sauté for about 3 minutes until slightly softened, then add the tomato and thyme. Stir and adjust the seasoning, if necessary. Reduce the heat to low and cook for 10–12 minutes until soft. Check the seasoning one more time.

2. Meanwhile, make the couscous. In a medium saucepan, bring 700ml water to the boil. Add the couscous, stir, cover and simmer for about 2 minutes until the water is absorbed. Fluff up with a fork, then turn off the heat, cover and leave to stand for 5 minutes. Fluff up again and then stir in the basil strips. Season with salt and pepper.

3. Fill a small ring mould, an emptied and thoroughly washed tuna can or a small rice bowl with the couscous and invert onto an individual serving plate. Repeat with three more serving plates. Alternatively, transfer the couscous to four pasta bowls. Top the couscous with the ratatouille, drizzle with the oil, garnish with the basil sprigs and serve.

TO DRINK:
A sparkling wine from the Loire Valley, like Charles de Fère Réserve Blanc de Blancs Brut

[Serves 4]

4 tablespoons extra-virgin olive oil, plus more for drizzling

1 small red onion, cut into 5mm dice

2 Japanese aubergines, or 1 small regular aubergine, unpeeled, cut into 1cm dice

sea salt and freshly ground black pepper

2 tablespoons finely chopped garlic

2 tablespoons fermented black beans

2 red peppers, deseeded and cut into 1cm dice

2 medium courgettes, cut into 1cm dice

170g tomatoes, preferably heirloom, cut into 1cm dice

2 tablespoons finely chopped fresh thyme

350g wholemeal couscous

8 Thai basil leaves, cut into thin strips, plus sprigs for garnish

2 tablespoons wheat-free tamari sauce

TO DRINK:
A Dolcetto d'Alba from Italy

[Serves 4]

3 tablespoons extra-virgin olive oil

1 tablespoon finely chopped garlic

250g wild mushrooms, such as oyster, chanterelles or shiitakes, individually or in combination, torn apart or thinly sliced, depending on size and shape

sea salt and freshly ground black pepper

25g unsalted butter

1 medium onion, finely chopped

475ml milk

950ml fresh chicken stock or stock made from low-salt chicken stock cubes

225g instant polenta

50g Parmigiano-Reggiano cheese, shaved or grated

30g Thai basil leaves or regular basil

grated zest of 1 lemon and juice of ½ lemon

1 teaspoon pink peppercorns, finger-crushed

wild mushroom polenta with thai basil salad

Mushrooms are the vegetarian meat. Their chewy texture and deep satisfying flavour – mushrooms are rich in *umami* – make this dish super-tasty. Next to rice, polenta is my favourite starch; it's particularly great when combined with mushrooms and paired with a sprightly basil salad. This all cooks very fast too, so it's a great dish to make when time is short.

1. Heat a medium saucepan over a medium heat. Add 2 tablespoons of the oil and swirl to coat the bottom. When the oil is hot, add the garlic and sauté, stirring, for about 1 minute until soft. Add the mushrooms and sauté for 3–4 minutes until lightly cooked. Season with salt and pepper. Transfer the mixture to a plate and set aside.

2. Add half the butter and the remaining tablespoon of oil to the pan. When the butter has melted, add the onions and sauté, stirring, for about 3 minutes until softened. Season with salt and pepper. Add the milk and stock and bring to a simmer. Whisking the liquid, add the polenta in a fine, steady stream, reduce the heat to low and cook, whisking from time to time, for 3–4 minutes until creamy and smooth. Adjust the seasoning, if necessary. Just before serving, whisk in the remaining butter, the cheese and the mushrooms.

3. In a small bowl, combine the basil and the lemon zest and juice. Season with salt and pepper and toss lightly. Transfer the polenta to four individual bowls, top with the basil salad, sprinkle with the pink peppercorns and serve.

Ming's Tip:

When shopping, buy the freshest mushrooms available, no matter the type. Always substitute when a specific ingredient doesn't measure up to a fresher one that can be used interchangeably.

sweet potato ravioli with brown thai basil butter

My good friend Mario Batali of Manhattan's award-winning Babbo restaurant inspired this dish. His delicious version pairs sweet potato ravioli with brown butter and sage; mine uses convenient wonton wrappers to make the ravioli and features Thai basil. A touch of honey and five-spice powder in the ravioli filling tilts my dish further towards the East. And speaking of the East, the Chinese did invent pasta, though if you cook as wonderfully as Mario, that's way beside the point.

1. Preheat the oven to 190°C/375°F/Gas Mark 5. Wrap the potatoes in foil, prick several times with a fork and bake for about 45 minutes until soft.

2. Scoop the potato flesh into a medium bowl. Add the five-spice powder, the larger quantity of chives and the honey. Season with salt and pepper.

3. When the filling has cooled, make the ravioli. Centre 1 basil leaf on 1 wonton wrapper, top with 1 tablespoon of the filling and top with a second basil leaf. Brush the edges of the wrapper with the egg mixture, top with a second wrapper and seal by pressing outwards along the edges with a finger. Repeat to make about 20 ravioli.

4. Line a large plate with kitchen paper. Add 25g of the butter to a large sauté pan and heat over a medium heat. When hot, add half the ravioli and sauté, turning once, for about 4 minutes until brown and crisp. Transfer the ravioli to the plate. Using another 25g butter, sauté the remaining ravioli and transfer to the plate. Divide the ravioli between four individual serving plates.

5. Add the remaining butter to the pan and cook for 2–3 minutes until the butter has browned lightly. Standing back to avoid any splatters, add the remaining basil and the vinegar and mix.

6. Drizzle the sauce over the ravioli, garnish with chives and serve.

TO DRINK:
A light Pinot Noir

[Serves 4 as a main course]

2 large sweet potatoes

1 teaspoon five-spice powder

1 bunch chives, finely sliced, 1 tablespoon reserved for garnish

2 tablespoons honey

sea salt and freshly ground black pepper

20g Thai basil leaves

one 350g packet square wonton wrappers

1 large egg mixed with 2 tablespoons water

115g unsalted butter

4 tablespoons balsamic vinegar

4

Think roasting and you probably picture a turkey served with 'trimmings' you've prepared separately. But there's an easier way. Following my one-pot approach, a 'main' item like pork, lamb or chicken is cooked with other ingredients to create a dish that's complete in itself. Dishes such as Ginger Chicken Thighs with Parsnips and Chilli Pork Fillets with Garlic Brussels Sprouts showcase this approach, which recasts the roasting tin as a kind of casserole.

One-pot roasting has other advantages. Once your dish is in the oven and you've set your timer, you can walk away from the cooker without needing to return until the dish is done. Kids ready to eat before the adults, or someone's detained? Serve some of your roast now and the rest will still be fine later. Roasting can be perfect for entertaining too. A dish like Miso-Marinated Lamb with Carrots and Potatoes can be started before guests arrive, then served with little last-minute attention. People think of roasting as 'big deal', but with my one-pot approach it's 'everyday'.

ROAST

orange-yuzu glazed chicken with wild rice salad

Yuzu juice, which comes from the Japanese citrus fruit, has a wonderfully intriguing flavour. It tastes like lemongrass and lime leaf combined, and it makes the chicken in this recipe exotically delicious. Yuzu is also used in the dressing for the wild rice accompaniment. I love wild rice, a grain some people think of as old-fashioned but that I call timeless. This makes a great company or weekend family dish.

1. To make the glaze, combine the orange juice, yuzu juice and honey in a small bowl. Season with salt and pepper. Remove 4 tablespoons of the mixture to a second small bowl and set both bowls aside.

2. Fill a large bowl with water and add ice. Cook the beans in abundant boiling water until tender-cripsp: 2–3 minutes for haricots verts, 4–5 minutes for regular beans. Using a large sieve, transfer the beans to the iced water. When cold, drain the beans. If using regular beans, cut them into 2.5cm lengths. Set the beans aside.

3. Preheat the oven to 190°C/375°F/Gas Mark 5. Season the chicken well with salt and pepper.

4. Heat a large, heavy ovenproof frying pan over a high heat. Add the oil and swirl to coat the bottom. When the oil is hot, add the chicken and cook, turning once, for 8–10 minutes until browned. Transfer the chicken to a platter and pour out all but 1 tablespoon of the fat. Reduce the heat to medium and add the onions. Season with salt and pepper and sauté, stirring, for 5–7 minutes until softened.

5. Return the chicken to the pan and brush with the glaze. Transfer to the oven, bake for 10 minutes and brush again with the glaze. Bake until the chicken is done, 20–25 minutes in all. Transfer the onions to a large bowl.

6. Meanwhile, in a small bowl, blend the orange zest, mustard, the reserved 4 tablespoons brushing syrup and the yogurt.

7. Add the rice and beans to the bowl with the onions. Add all but 2 tablespoons of the mustard-yogurt mixture and toss lightly. Season with salt and pepper.

8. Carve the chicken. Transfer the rice salad to four individual plates and add a dollop of the remaining mustard-yogurt mixture to one side.

TO DRINK:
A Crisp Loire Valley wine,
New Zealand Sauvignon Blanc
or Prosecco like Cantina Produttori
de Valdobbiadene Val d'Oca

[Serves 4]

2 tablespoons orange juice and grated zest of ½ orange

2 tablespoons yuzu juice or naturally brewed ponzu

170g honey

sea salt and freshly ground black pepper

ice cubes

225g haricots verts or regular French beans, stem-ends trimmed

one 2.7kg chicken, split, washed and patted dry

2 tablespoons grapeseed or rapeseed oil

2 red onions, cut into 2.5cm slices

1 tablespoon Dijon mustard

125ml Greek yogurt

330g cooked wild rice (see page 12); save extra rice for another use

Ming's Tip:

You can make the glaze ahead of time and store it in a lidded plastic container in the fridge.

TO DRINK:

A Californian Shiraz or Syrah

[Serves 4]

900g chicken thighs, skin on

sea salt and freshly ground black pepper

3 tablespoons grapeseed or rapeseed oil

2 large onions, cut into 2.5cm dice

2 tablespoons finely chopped fresh ginger

3 large parsnips, peeled and roll-cut into
2.5cm lengths (see page 13) or
cut conventionally

4 celery sticks, roll-cut into 2.5cm lengths
(see page 13) or cut conventionally

5 sprigs fresh thyme

ginger
chicken thighs
with parsnips

Chicken thighs are my favourite part of the bird. They've got just the right meat-to-skin ratio and they really shine in this quick, gingery bake that's great for post-work cooking. This dish also features parsnips, which I think of as white carrots. They're as sweet as carrots but have more character.

1. Preheat the oven to 230°C/450°F/Gas Mark 8.

2. Season the thighs with the salt and pepper. Heat a large, heavy roasting tin or heavy frying pan over a medium-high heat. Add 2 tablespoons of the oil and swirl to coat the bottom. When the oil is hot, add the thighs skin side down. Cook for about 10 minutes, turning once, until browned. Transfer the thighs to a platter and set aside.

3. Add the remaining oil to the pan, swirl and heat. When the oil is hot, add the onions, ginger, parsnips, celery and thyme. Season with salt and pepper and sauté the vegetables, stirring, for about 6 minutes until softened. Top with the thighs, skin side up, and bake uncovered for 30–40 minutes until the chicken and vegetables are done. Transfer to a platter or four individual serving plates and serve.

mushroom chicken fricassee with edamame

TO DRINK:
A Californian Pinot Noir

[Serves 4]

Everyone loves homey chicken fricassee – and my version is super-easy, as well as delicious. You brown the chicken – legs plus thighs, the most flavourful parts of the bird – add mushrooms and aromatics, liquid and edamame, and bake. In about 40 minutes you have a great, savoury meal. This is a terrific dish for after-work cooking, of course, but I find myself making it even if I have spare time.

900g chicken legs with thighs, skin on

sea salt and freshly ground black pepper

2 tablespoons grapeseed or rapeseed oil

1 large red onion, halved and sliced 5mm thick

1 tablespoon finely chopped garlic

450g mushrooms, sliced 5mm thick

2 tablespoons finely chopped fresh tarragon

500g canned whole Italian plum tomatoes, roughly chopped, with the juice from measuring

150g shelled edamame

1. Preheat the oven to 200°C/400°F/Gas Mark 6. Season the chicken with salt and pepper.

2. Heat a large roasting tin or large, heavy ovenproof frying pan over a medium-high heat. Add the oil and swirl to coat the bottom. When the oil is hot, add the chicken and sauté, turning once, for about 20 minutes until browned. Transfer to a plate and set aside.

3. Drain the pan of all but 1 tablespoon of the fat. Add the onions, garlic and mushrooms and sauté for 2–3 minutes until lightly browned. Season with salt and pepper. Add the tarragon, tomatoes with their juice and edamame. Mix well and adjust the seasoning, if necessary. Top with the chicken, transfer to the oven and bake for 20–25 minutes until the chicken is cooked through. Transfer to a platter and serve.

TO DRINK:
An Australian Pinot Noir

[Serves 4]

8 duck legs (legs plus thighs)

sea salt and freshly ground black pepper

2 tablespoons grapeseed or rapeseed oil

2 rashers thick-cut back bacon

2 medium onions, thickly sliced

six 1cm-thick slices peeled fresh ginger, cut lengthways from a 5–10cm piece

1 serrano chilli, halved lengthways

3 medium oranges, quartered

130g trimmed baby carrots, or peeled regular carrots cut into chunks

4 celery sticks, cut into 1cm lengths

300g shelled edamame

125ml Grand Marnier or other orange liqueur

4 tablespoons naturally brewed soy sauce

475ml fresh chicken stock or stock made from a low-salt chicken stock cube

ginger-orange duck 'cassoulet'

I love duck legs, sold as leg-thigh combos. They're not only incredibly tasty but are easier to handle than a whole duck, which often needs to be jointed before cooking. Like traditional cassoulet, this is a great one-pot meal. However, it uses edamame instead of the customary heavier beans, and it features the bright freshness of orange. Serve this with good bread.

1. Preheat the oven to 180°C/350°F/Gas Mark 4.

2. Season the duck legs with salt and pepper. Heat a large flameproof casserole dish over a medium heat, add the oil and swirl to coat the bottom. When the oil is hot, and working in batches if necessary, add the duck legs skin side down. Cook, turning once, for about 20 minutes until browned. If the legs haven't rendered most of their fat, cook a little longer. Transfer the legs to a plate and pour off all the fat (reserve the fat for future use).

3. Add the bacon, onions, ginger and chilli. Season with salt and pepper and sauté for about 2 minutes until the vegetables have softened slightly. Add the oranges, carrots, celery and edamame and deglaze the pan with the Grand Marnier. Add the soy sauce and stock and adjust the seasoning if necessary. Return the duck legs to the casserole, cover and transfer to the oven. Bake for about 2 hours until a paring knife passes easily through the duck. Serve from the casserole or transfer to a large shallow bowl and serve.

TO DRINK:
A Californian Pinot Noir

[Serves 4]

675g fresh chicken sausages
(see page 11)

150g coriander seeds, coarsely ground
(see Ming's Tip)

2 tablespoons grapeseed or rapeseed oil

2 medium onions, cut into 2.5cm dice

3 fennel bulbs, halved, cored and sliced
5mm thick

3 celery sticks, cut into 2.5cm dice

sea salt and freshly ground black pepper

370g jasmine rice, or 185g jasmine and
185g brown rice

950ml fresh chicken stock or stock made
from low-salt chicken stock cubes

Ming's Tip:

Use a heavy pan and chopping board
to crush the coriander seeds.

If you make this following the
jasmine plus brown rice option,
the brown rice will cook up a bit
chewier than the jasmine, providing
textural interest.

chicken sausage with fennel rice pilaf

As a pork-sausage lover, I used to scoff at chicken sausage. Now I know better. Buy quality chicken sausages and you get spicy, unctuous eating equal to that of the pork kind. In this dish, chicken sausages are made into coriander-scented meatballs that are baked with fennel and jasmine or brown rice – or, my preference, a half-half combination. This is delicious eating and is a particularly great dish for easy entertaining.

1. Preheat the oven to 190°C/375°F/Gas Mark 5. Remove the sausagemeat from the casings and roll into 1cm balls.

2. Place the coriander seeds on a large shallow plate, add the sausage balls and turn to coat with the coriander. Heat a flameproof casserole dish or large, heavy saucepan over a high heat, add the oil and swirl to coat the bottom. When the oil is hot, add the sausage balls and sauté on all sides for about 6 minutes until brown. Transfer the balls to a plate and set aside.

3. Reduce the heat to medium. Add the onions, fennel and celery to the pan and season with salt and pepper. Sauté, stirring, for about 8 minutes until browned. Add the rice, stir to combine and add the sausage balls. Add the stock and bring to a simmer. Cover, transfer the pan to the oven and bake for 40 minutes until the rice is cooked. Remove the pan from the oven and leave to stand, covered, for 15 minutes. Serve from the pan or transfer the mixture to a platter and serve.

jerk chicken with mango

TO DRINK:
Dark and Stormy cocktails

Several theories exist about how jerk chicken got its name. The one I was first told, and that I'll stick with, links the name with the practice of jerking – poking – holes in the meat for spice-filling before the bird is cooked. It's a wonderful dish no matter its name's derivation, especially when paired with mangoes that have been cooked until caramelised and chewy. Jerk chicken is traditionally served with French fries. All I can say is, knock yourself out!

1. Make the marinade a day in advance. Using a mortar and pestle, or in a small food processor, combine the garlic, ginger, thyme, five-spice powder, black pepper, sambal, orange zest, 1 tablespoon of the sugar and the salt and purée. Add the orange juice and oil and combine.

2. Coat the chicken inside and out with the jerk paste and leave to marinate, covered and refrigerated, overnight.

3. Preheat the oven to 240°C/475°F/Gas Mark 9. In a small bowl,combine the mangoes, remaining sugar and the lime juice. Toss to coat the mangoes.

4. Transfer the chicken to a roasting tin and roast, rotating the pan once, for 25–35 minutes until the chicken has browned. Reduce the oven to 160°C/325°F/Gas Mark 3, tent lightly with foil and continue to roast the chicken for about a further 1 hour. About 20 minutes before the chicken is done, add the mangoes to the pan and cook until caramelised.

5. Transfer the chicken to a chopping board and leave to rest 10 minutes. Transfer the chicken to a platter, surround with the mangoes, carve at the table and serve.

[Serves 4]

6 garlic cloves, peeled

2 tablespoons finely chopped fresh ginger

2 tablespoons finely chopped fresh thyme

2 tablespoons five-spice powder

1 tablespoon freshly ground black pepper

2 tablespoons sambal, or 1 small habernero or Scotch bonnet chilli, finely chopped

grated zest and juice of 1 large orange

2 tablespoons soft dark brown sugar

1 tablespoon sea salt

4 tablespoons grapeseed or rapeseed oil

one 2.25–2.7kg chicken

2 mangoes, stoned, peeled and cut into wedges

juice of 1 lime

TO DRINK:
An unoaked Californian Chardonnay

cranberry-hoisin chicken 'n' rice

[Serves 4]

2 tablespoons grapeseed or rapeseed oil

8 chicken thighs, skin on

sea salt and freshly ground black pepper

2 tablespoons finely chopped garlic

2 bunches spring onions, thinly sliced

370g jasmine rice

4 tablespoons hoisin sauce

225ml dry red wine

95g fresh cranberries

700ml fresh chicken stock or stock made from low-salt chicken stock cubes

I've always loved the chicken-with-rice dishes of Singapore, which are riffs on poached chicken served on savoury rice. My one-pot version shouts chicken flavour, as the rice is sautéed in chicken fat before it's baked. I love tasty chicken fat, but if you're concerned about its healthfulness, remove most of it from the casserole before adding the aromatics. Tart cranberries balance the richness of the dish while taming the sweetness of the hoisin. This is a perfect dish for entertaining.

1. Preheat the oven to 190°C/375°F/Gas Mark 5.

2. Choose a large flameproof casserole dish with a tight-fitting lid and place the casserole over a medium-high heat. Add the oil and swirl to coat the bottom. When the oil is hot, add the chicken, in batches if necessary. Season with salt and pepper and sauté on all sides for about 8 minutes until lightly coloured. Transfer to a plate and set aside.

3. Add the garlic and spring onions to the casserole dish and sauté, stirring, for 1 minute. Add the rice and sauté, stirring, for 1 minute. Add the hoisin sauce and sauté for 30 seconds. Add the wine, deglaze and simmer for about 2 minutes until the liquid is reduced by three quarters. Add the cranberries and stock and season with salt and pepper. Return the chicken to the casserole and bring to a simmer.

4. Cover the dish, transfer to the oven and cook for 20–30 minutes until the chicken is tender and the rice is cooked. Remove from the oven and leave to rest for 10 minutes. Bring the pan to the table and serve.

moroccan spiced lamb with red pepper couscous

TO DRINK:
A rich, high-quality Bordeaux

Visiting Morocco I became aware of the great job done there with 'lesser' meat cuts, like lamb shoulder. The shoulder has great flavour and good fat content – and when marinated overnight, it cooks up tasty as well as tender. The secret is a full-flavoured marinade, which it gets here. The lamb is also roasted on a bed of onions, which pick up the savouriness of the lamb fat and juice. Served with couscous, the traditional Moroccan accompaniment, this is a feast.

[Serves 4]

1. In a medium bowl, combine the thyme, garlic, coriander, coarsely ground black pepper, cumin, fennel, cinnamon, paprika, honey, chilli powder and 1 tablespoon salt. Add the olive oil, reserving the 2 tablespoons, and stir to blend. Transfer 125ml of the mixture to a serving bowl and refrigerate, covered. Coat both sides of the lamb with the remaining mixture and transfer to a large resealable plastic bag. Marinate, refrigerated, for at least 2 hours or overnight.

2. Preheat the oven to 240°C/475°F/Gas Mark 9. Place the onions in a roasting tin and season with salt and pepper. Top with the lamb, transferring any remaining marinade to a bowl, and roast for about 15 minutes until browned.

3. Reduce the heat to 190°C/375°F/Gas Mark 5. Turn the lamb, brush on the remaining marinade and roast for 20–25 minutes or until a meat thermometer inserted in the thickest part of the meat registers 49°C/120°F for medium-rare, 54.5°C/130°F for medium or 60°C/140°F for medium-well. Transfer the onions to a medium bowl, and the lamb to a chopping board to rest for 10 minutes.

4. Meanwhile, make the couscous. Bring 700ml salted water to the boil in a medium saucepan. Add the couscous, drizzle with the 2 tablespoons oil and stir. Remove from the heat, cover and leave to stand for 4–5 minutes until the couscous has absorbed the water. Fluff up with a fork. Add the red peppers and stir lightly to blend.

5. Slice the lamb thinly on the bias. Serve with the couscous, onions and the reserved marinade.

2 tablespoons finely chopped fresh thyme

4 tablespoons finely chopped garlic

2 tablespoons coarsely ground coriander seeds

2 tablespoons coarsely ground black pepper

2 tablespoons coarsely ground cumin seeds

2 tablespoons coarsely ground fennel seeds

1 tablespoon ground cinnamon

1 tablespoon paprika

2 tablespoons honey

1 tablespoon ancho chilli powder, or other chilli powder

1 tablespoon Sea salt, plus more for seasoning

225ml extra-virgin olive oil, 2 tablespoons reserved

one 2.25–2.7kg boned lamb shoulder, spread flat

3 large onions, cut lengthways 5mm thick

freshly ground black pepper

350g couscous

3 red peppers, deseeded and cut into 5mm dice

wine and black bean pot roast with smashed potatoes

Pot roast is a grandmotherly dish with many variations, depending, usually, on where one's grandmother – or great-grandmother – came from. China is my answer, so my version uses fermented black beans for deep, enticing flavour. Technically, this is a shallow braise, but I hope you'll allow me a little culinary licence because the beef is actually baked, very slowly, to doneness. Rough-textured smashed potatoes – some people call them mashed 'country-style' – complete the meal.

1. Preheat the oven to 120°C/250°F/Gas Mark ½. Wrap the potatoes in foil and pierce several times with a fork. Set aside.

2. Season the beef generously with salt and pepper. Heat a large flameproof casserole or heavy roasting tin over a medium-high heat. Add the oil and swirl to coat the bottom. When the oil is hot, add the beef and sauté on all sides for about 15 minutes until browned. Transfer the beef to a plate and set aside.

3. Pour off all but 2 tablespoons of the fat from the pan. Add the beans, garlic, ginger and spring oinons and sauté for about 2 minutes until softened. Add the wine, deglaze the pan and cook for 5–6 minutes to reduce the liquid by half. Add the stock, carrots, rosemary and soy sauce, stir and season with salt and pepper. Cover the casserole, or if using a roasting tin, cover tightly with foil. Transfer to the oven and cook for about 4 hours until a fork passes easily through the meat. After 2¹/₂ hours of cooking, place the potatoes in the oven.

4. Remove the casserole and potatoes and leave the meat to stand in its liquid, covered, for 20 minutes. Transfer the roast to a carving board and leave to rest for 5 minutes. Meanwhile, transfer the casserole with the braising liquid to the hob and reduce the liquid over a high heat for about 5 minutes.

5. Slice half the roast 3mm thick and transfer the slices plus the remaining half to the casserole. Spoon the potatoes into a medium bowl and mash roughly. Bring the casserole and potatoes to the table and serve.

TO DRINK:
A big red wine from Chile, like Montes Purple Angel Carmenere

[Serves 4]

8 medium Yukon Gold or Estima potatoes

one 3.6–4.5kg piece silverside or brisket

sea salt and freshly ground black pepper

2 tablespoons grapeseed or rapeseed oil

2 tablespoons finely chopped fermented black beans

2 tablespoons finely chopped garlic

1 tablespoon finely chopped fresh ginger

1 bunch spring onions, thinly sliced

1 bottle red wine

950ml fresh chicken stock or stock made from low-salt chicken stock cubes

450g trimmed baby carrots, or peeled regular carrots, cut into chunks

2 sprigs fresh rosemary

4 tablespoons naturally brewed soy sauce

Ming's Tip:

You can use a large slow cooker to make this. Once everything is added to the pot, count on about 6 hours for the dish to be done.

miso-marinated lamb racks with carrots and potatoes

When you're cooking for a special occasion and can blow a little cash to make something really great, lamb racks are the thing. I prefer New Zealand racks for their smaller eyes and 'gamier' taste, but truthfully, I've never met a lamb rack I didn't like. In this dish the lamb racks are marinated in a miso-sake mixture that gives them enticing taste, then roasted with potatoes and carrots. This is 'one-pot' cooking that's easy as well as elegant.

1. In a large bowl, combine the miso, shallots, wasabi, sugar and sake and stir to blend. Whisk in the oil and blend. Set aside 4 tablespoons of the marinade.

2. Add the lamb racks to the bowl, turn to coat them, cover and leave to marinate, refrigerated, for 2–4 hours.

3. Preheat the oven to 200°C/400°F/Gas Mark 6. Choose a heavy roasting tin or heavy ovenproof frying pan large enough to hold the racks and heat in the oven for about 10 minutes until very hot. Meanwhile, in a medium bowl combine the potatoes, carrots, spring onion whites and reserved marinade. Toss and season with salt and pepper.

4. Open the oven, pull out the oven rack with the pan and add the potato mixture. The mixture will sizzle. Top with the lamb racks and roast until a meat thermometer inserted in the thickest part of the meat registers 46–47.8°C/115–118°F for medium-rare, 15–20 minutes. (Or use a knife to determine doneness, see Ming's Tip.) Remove the racks and leave them to rest for 10 minutes. Transfer the potato mixture to a platter, top with the racks, garnish with the spring onion greens and serve.

TO DRINK:
A Californian Bordeaux blend

[Serves 4]

125g shiro miso

2 large shallots, finely chopped

1 tablespoon rehydrated wasabi powder or wasabi paste

1 tablespoon sugar

125ml sake

125ml grapeseed or rapeseed oil

2 lamb racks (about 900g each)

2 large Yukon Gold or Estima potatoes, unpeeled, washed and cut into 2.5cm dice

450g trimmed baby carrots, or peeled regular carrots, cut into chunks

100g spring onions, finely sliced, white and green parts separated

sea salt and freshly ground black pepper

Ming's Tip:

To test the racks for doneness, insert a paring knife into the thickest part of the meat, remove it and touch its tip to your lower lip. If the knife is cool, the meat is rare; if not quite warm, medium-rare; if warm, medium; if hot, medium-well.

TO DRINK:
*A big buttery California
Central Coast Chardonnay*

[Serves 4]

55g sea salt, for brining, plus more
for seasoning

4 tablespoons granulated sugar

four 225g pork fillets cut from the loin

3 tablespoons ancho chilli powder, or
other chilli powder

2 tablespoons soft dark brown sugar

4 tablespoons finely chopped garlic

55g unsalted butter, melted

freshly ground black pepper

3 tablespoons grapeseed or rapeseed oil

550g Brussels sprouts, halved and cored

10 new potatoes, halved

2 tablespoons naturally brewed ponzu

chilli pork fillets with garlic brussels sprouts

Pork is my favourite meat – and fillets cut from the loin are a great way to enjoy it. The meat's sweetness is yin to the yang of chilli in this delicious recipe, which also features garlicky Brussels sprouts. I wasn't always a fan of that vegetable, but now I am, having enjoyed them properly prepared, as they are here. Cooked until just done, the sprouts have a delicate cabbage flavour that even kids will love. This versatile dish works for family and company alike.

1. At least 2 and up to 4 hours in advance, brine the pork. In a bowl large enough to hold the pork and brine, combine the brining salt, granulated sugar and 1.9 litres water. Stir to dissolve the salt and sugar and add the pork. If the pork isn't covered, add more water. Refrigerate for 2–4 hours. Rinse the pork and pat dry.

2. Preheat the oven to 180°C/350°F/Gas Mark 4. On a large shallow plate, blend together the chilli powder, brown sugar, 2 tablespoons of the garlic and the butter. Roll the pork in the mixture and season lightly with salt and pepper.

3. Heat a large, heavy ovenproof frying pan over a medium heat. Add 2 table-spoons of the oil and swirl to coat the pan. When the oil is hot, add the pork and sauté, turning once, for about 6 minutes until browned. Transfer the pork to a plate and set aside.

4. Add the remaining tablespoon of oil to the frying pan, swirl, and when hot, add the Brussels sprouts, potatoes, remaining garlic and ponzu. Season with salt and pepper and mix well. Top with the pork and roast in the oven for 15–20 minutes until the pork is medium, with an internal temperature of 40°C/140°F. Remove and leave to rest 10 minutes.

5. Transfer the sprouts and potatoes to four individual plates, top with the pork and serve. Alternatively, transfer the pork to a chopping board and slice. Divide the vegetables and sliced pork between four individual serving plates and serve.

five-spice honey pork tenderloin with leeks

TO DRINK:
A French Pinot Noir

Pork is surely the sweetest meat – and the honey-mustard glaze given it in this recipe enhances that pleasing virtue. Leeks, which I think of as French spring onions, add a subtle sweetness of their own, and five-spice powder, often used with pork in Chinese cooking, adds its distinctive warmth. This delicious dish is perfect for entertaining.

1. At least 2 and up to 4 hours in advance, brine the pork. In a bowl large enough to hold the pork and brine, combine the brining salt, sugar and 1.9 litres water. Stir to dissolve the salt and sugar and add the pork. If the pork isn't covered, add more water. Refrigerate for 2–4 hours.

2. Preheat the oven to 200°C/400°F/Gas Mark 6. Season the leeks with salt and pepper and transfer to a medium bowl. In a small bowl, combine the five-spice powder, mustard and honey. Pour about one third of the mixture into a second small bowl and set both bowls aside.

3. Rinse the pork well, pat dry and season lightly with salt and more generously with pepper. Heat a large, heavy ovenproof frying pan over a high heat. Add the grapeseed oil and swirl to coat the bottom. When the oil is hot, add the pork and sauté on all sides for about 8 minutes until browned. Transfer the pork to a plate.

4. Add the olive oil to the pan, swirl, and when hot, add the leeks. Sauté, stirring, for about 3 minutes until soft. Add the rice and stock to the pan and stir. Top with the pork, brush with some of the larger quantity of the honey glaze and roast the pork for 10 minutes. Turn the pork, brush again with the glaze and roast for 10–15 minutes until just cooked through, or to an internal temperature of 65.5°C/150°F. (Alternatively, insert a paring knife into the thickest part of the meat. If the juices run clear and the knife feels hot, the pork is done.)

5. Transfer the pork to a carving board and leave to rest for 8–10 minutes. Slice the pork 5mm thick. Transfer the leek mixture to a platter, top with the pork, drizzle with the reserved glaze and serve.

[Serves 4]

2 medium pork tenderloins (about 900g), any silverskin removed

55g sea salt, for brining, plus more for seasoning

4 tablespoons sugar

2 large leeks, white parts cut into 1cm dice, well washed and dried (see Ming's Tip on washing, page 47)

freshly ground black pepper

1 teaspoon five-spice powder

2 tablespoons Dijon mustard

170g honey

2 tablespoons grapeseed or rapeseed oil

2 tablespoons extra-virgin olive oil

490g cooked wild rice (see page 12)

125ml fresh chicken stock or stock made from a low-salt chicken stock cube

peppered pork tenderloin with coconut cranberry sauce

It's no secret that pork and fruit make a great duo. This dish pairs peppery pork with extra-tart dried cranberries and ponzu, and adds the taste of coconut. I use coconut milk here because it provides richness as well as great flavour. In fact, whenever I'm about to reach for cream to add to a dish, I think coconut milk, and I often use it instead. It has the same mouthfeel as cream and adds exotic flavour. This is another perfect dish for entertaining.

1. At least 2 and up to 4 hours in advance, brine the pork. In a bowl large enough to hold the pork and brine, combine the brining salt, sugar and 1.9 litres water. Stir to dissolve the salt and sugar and add the pork. If the pork isn't covered, add more water and refrigerate for 2–4 hours.

2. Preheat the oven to 230°C/450°F/Gas Mark 8. Bake the sweet potatoes for about 40 minutes until they are soft. Do not turn off the oven.

3. About 15 minutes before the potatoes are done, rinse the pork and pat dry. Season lightly with salt and coat with the pepper. Heat an ovenproof sauté pan over a medium heat. Add the oil and swirl to coat the bottom. When hot, add the pork and sauté on all sides for 2–3 minutes. Transfer the pan to the oven and roast for 6–8 minutes for medium or to an internal temperature of 65.5°C/150°F. (You can also determine doneness by inserting a knife into the thickest part of the pork; see Ming's Tip, page 118.) Remove the pork to a chopping board to rest.

4. Add a touch more oil to the pan and swirl to coat the bottom. When the oil is hot, add the onions and dried cranberries and sauté, stirring, for 4–5 minutes until the onions have browned lightly. Add the ponzu, deglaze the pan and cook for about 1 minute until the liquid is reduced by half. Whisk in the coconut milk and butter and season with salt and pepper.

5. Cut the pork into 12 slices. Divide the sauce between four individual serving plates. Scoop out the potato flesh from its skin and divide it between the plates. Surround each scoop of potato with 3 slices of pork and serve.

TO DRINK:
A crisp, off-dry Australian Riesling

[Serves 4]

2 medium pork tenderloins (about 900g), any silverskin removed

55g sea salt, for brining, plus more for seasoning

4 tablespoons sugar

2 medium sweet potatoes

2 tablespoons coarsely ground black pepper

2 tablespoons grapeseed or rapeseed oil, plus more as needed

1 large red onion, finely chopped

60g dried cranberries, coarsely chopped

125ml naturally brewed ponzu

one 400g can coconut milk, shaken

15g unsalted butter

TO DRINK:
A chilled India Pale Ale, like Samual Adams or Greene King IPA

[Serves 4]

sea salt

300g Israeli couscous

1 tablespoon finely chopped garlic

1 tablespoon finely chopped fresh ginger

1 teaspoon sambal, or other hot sauce

4 tablespoons hoisin sauce

grated zest and juice of 1 large lemon

two 400g packs firm tofu, quartered lengthways

4 tablespoons extra-virgin olive oil

1 large summer squash or 2–3 fat courgettes, cut into 3mm slices

1 large tomato, cut into 5mm dice

1 bunch spring onions, white and green parts, thinly sliced

freshly ground black pepper

barbecued tofu with israeli couscous salad

Barbecuing isn't just for hamburgers. For this easy dish, tofu is brushed with a garlicky hoisin-based 'barbecue sauce', then grilled until the surface is deliciously caramelised. I pair the tofu with Israeli couscous, which, if you haven't tried it, is pearl-grained and has a satisfying tender-chewy texture. The couscous is enlivened with thinly sliced raw squash, spring onions and tomatoes, and is served with the glazed tofu on top.

1. To make the couscous, bring 950ml salted water to the boil in a medium saucepan. Stir in the couscous, lower the heat to medium and cook, stirring frequently, for 5–10 minutes until the couscous is tender. Remove from the heat, transfer to a large sieve and cool under cold running water. Set aside.

2. Preheat the grill. In a large bowl, combine the garlic, ginger, sambal, hoisin and lemon zest and stir to blend. Place the tofu on a baking sheet and brush generously with the hoisin mixture. Transfer the remaining hoisin mixture to a large bowl.

3. Grill the tofu at the middle level for about 6 minutes until the surface has caramelised and the tofu is heated through.

4. Meanwhile, whisk the oil and lemon juice into the reserved hoisin mixture. Add the squash, tomato, spring onions and couscous, toss and season with salt and pepper. Transfer the salad to four individual serving plates, top each portion with two parallel slices of tofu and serve.

5

My high-temperature cooking involves two techniques: flash-frying and steaming. These one-pot methods differ from other hob techniques in the way that heat is transferred to raw ingredients – indirectly, that is, via vapour or hot oil. I'm particularly fond of high-temp recipes, as they produce some of cooking's most delectable dishes. Everyone loves crunch, and 'hot oil' dishes such as Spicy Fried Chicken and Flash-Fried Aubergine with Honey-Lemon Syrup definitely prove the point.

Steaming is an under-explored technique in the West, but not in the East, where it's used in deliciously creative ways to produce dishes of fresh taste and appearance. The Chinese in particular have recognised the potential for 'one-pot' steaming, employing multi-tiered bamboo steamers to cook separate ingredients at once. My steamed recipes, like Lion's Head and Snow Cabbage with Brown Rice, reveal the deep pleasures – and convenience – of steam cooking. In fact, if I had my way, I'd make sure every household had a steamer and used it. Once you crank it up and add your ingredients, a delicious meal is just minutes away.

HIGH TEMP

spicy fried chicken
with crispy onion rings

Whenever I eat in the South in the US, I marvel at the number of ways chicken can be fried. Being a chef, I set out to make my own 'best' version. This is it – spicy, crisp and delicious, and super-moist because the bird is brined in buttermilk before frying. And you get crispy onion rings with your chicken, so the best's even better.

1. Brine the chicken a day in advance: Mix the brining salt, sugar and buttermilk together in a large bowl and stir to dissolve the sugar. Add the chicken, cover and refrigerate. Four hours before frying, add the onion rings, cover and refrigerate.

2. Remove the chicken from the brine and drain the onion rings on kitchen paper. Reserve the brine.

3. Set up a deep-fat fryer or use a heavy-based tall, wide saucepan. Add 2.5cm of the oil and heat to 160°C/325°F, as measured with a deep-fat thermometer. Meanwhile, on a large platter combine the chilli flakes, garlic and onion powders, paprika, cornflour and flour. Dredge the chicken in the cornflour mixture. Reserve the mixture.

4. Working in batches, shake any excess cornflour mixture from the chicken. Using a skimmer or tongs, lower the chicken into the oil. Fry the chicken for 12–14 minutes until golden brown and cooked through, turning as needed. Remove from the oil, season with salt and keep warm.

5. Allow the oil to reheat. Dredge the onion in the reserved flour mixture, dip in the brine and dredge again in the flour mixture. Add the onion rings to the oil and fry for about 3 minutes until golden brown. Drain the rings on kitchen paper and season lightly with salt. Transfer the chicken and onion rings to four individual serving plates and serve with the lemon for squeezing over.

TO DRINK:
Yanjing beer or other light, crisp lagers, such as Michelob Ultra, Corona or Stella Artois

[Serves 4]

80g sea salt, for brining, plus more for seasoning

100g sugar

950ml buttermilk

6 chicken legs and 6 thighs, skin on

1 large onion, cut into 1cm slices

grapeseed or rapeseed oil, for frying

2 tablespoons Korean red chilli flakes or chilli powder

2 tablespoons natural garlic powder

2 tablespoons onion powder

1 tablespoon paprika

250g cornflour

280g plain flour

1 lemon, quartered

Ming's Tip:
Salt the bird right after it's fried or the seasoning won't stick. And to ensure even salting, `rain' it on the bird from shoulder height.

panko-crusted turkey 'scaloppini' with warm mango-cranberry chutney

TO DRINK:
A Dolcetto d'Alba from Italy

I'm a great fan of turkey and constantly looking for new ways to serve it other than roasted. When making veal scaloppini one day, I suddenly wondered if I could substitute turkey for the veal. Turns out, turkey does beautifully pounded into thin slices, coated with breadcrumbs – here, Japanese panko – and quickly sautéed. When accompanied by warm mango-cranberry chutney, a recasting of the usual cranberry sauce, the scaloppini really shine.

[Serves 4]

900g skinless turkey breast, cut on the extreme bias into 8 slices about 20cm long and 1cm thick

sea salt and freshly ground black pepper

2 eggs

60g panko (Japanese breadcrumbs)

30g finely chopped parsley

140g plain flour

5 tablespoons extra-virgin olive oil

2 shallots, finely chopped

95g fresh cranberries, washed and dried

1 large mango, stoned, peeled and cut into 1cm dice

1 tablespoon Dijon mustard

1. Place a turkey portion on a work surface and cover with clingfilm. Using a meat mallet or small sauté pan, pound the turkey until 5mm thick. Repeat with the remaining portions. Season the turkey on both sides with salt and pepper.

2. In a shallow bowl, beat the eggs lightly. On a large plate, combine the panko and half the parsley. Spread the flour on a second plate.

3. One by one, coat the turkey portions lightly with the flour, dip them into the egg and then coat with the panko mixture.

4. Line a large plate with kitchen paper. Heat a large sauté pan over a medium-high heat. Add 2 tablespoons of the oil and swirl to coat the bottom. When the oil is hot, add half the turkey slices and sauté, turning once, for 6–8 minutes until golden brown and cooked through. Transfer the turkey to the plate. Repeat using 2 more tablespoons of the oil.

5. Wipe out the pan with kitchen paper and add the remaining tablespoon of oil. Swirl to coat the bottom, and when the oil is hot, add the shallots and sauté for about 1 minute until soft. Add the cranberries, mango and mustard and sauté, stirring, for about 2 minutes until the fruit is soft. Add the remaining parsley and stir to combine.

6. Transfer two scaloppini to each of four individual serving plates. Dollop some chutney on the side and serve.

TO DRINK:
A spicy dry Riesling, like Lucien Albrecht Reserve from France

[Serves 4]

675g pork shoulder, cut into 2.5cm cubes

sea salt and freshly ground black pepper

130g cornflour

125ml grapeseed or rapeseed oil

125ml naturally brewed rice vinegar

1–3 tablespoons sugar, depending on the mangoes' sweetness

1 bunch spring onions, thinly sliced, white and green parts separated

1 tablespoon finely chopped garlic

1 tablespoon finely chopped fresh ginger

1 medium red onion, cut into 5mm dice

2 small mangoes, stoned, peeled and cut into 1cm dice

1 red pepper, deseeded and cut into 5mm dice

4 tablespoons naturally brewed soy sauce

–

50-50 White and Brown Rice, for serving (see page 12)

sweet and sour mango pork

Almost anyone who's ever eaten Chinese food has had sweet and sour pork. Here's my tropical version, which should be a revelation to those who haven't always loved the dish. The key here is flash-frying the pork before combining it with the other ingredients, a technique that gives the meat crispness. Mango provides tropical allure, but if you can't find mangoes that are ripe, substitute a small pineapple. The result will be less exotic, but just as good.

1. Season the pork with salt and pepper. Spread the cornflour on a platter and dredge the pork thoroughly on all sides.

2. Line a large plate with kitchen paper. Heat a wok over a high heat. Add the oil and swirl to coat the pan. When the oil is hot, add half the pork and fry, turning the pork, for about 4 mintues until browned. Using a skimmer, transfer the pork to the lined plate to drain. Fry the remaining pork and transfer it to the plate. Pour off all but 1 tablespoon of the oil from the wok.

3. In a small bowl, combine the vinegar and sugar and stir to dissolve the sugar. Set aside.

4. Return the wok to a medium-high heat, and when the oil is hot, add the spring onion whites, garlic, ginger and red onion and stir-fry for about 1 minute until softened. And the mangoes, red pepper, soy sauce and vinegar mixture and bring to a simmer. Return the pork to the wok and mix thoroughly.

5. Transfer the stir-fry to a platter and serve with the rice.

lion's head and snow cabbage with house rice

Chinese dishes have evocative names. The lion's head of this recipe title refers to plus-size meatballs, here a savoury mixture of beef and pork mince, and the snow cabbage represents the mane. My grandfather would prepare the traditional version of this dish, which I've made even more savoury by adding, among other things, Worcestershire sauce, an under-appreciated seasoning. A final touch of sambal provides heat.

1. Set up a steamer, using an elevated bamboo steamer in a water-filled wok, a collapsible steamer well elevated above water or a commercial steamer with pan and steamer insert.

2. In a large bowl, combine the pork, beef, onions, garlic, ginger, Worcestershire sauce, sesame oil, rice and eggs. Season with salt and pepper and mix by hand until just combined. Check the seasoning by sautéing a small amount of the mixture, or use a microwave to cook it (about 10 seconds at high power).

3. Using your hands, lightly form the mixture into 5m balls. Place a 2–2.5cm bed of the cabbage in the top of the steamer and top with the meatballs. Season with salt and pepper and steam for 8–10 minutes until the meatballs and cabbage are cooked through. Transfer the cabbage to a platter or four serving plates, top with the meatballs, garnish with a bit of sambal and serve.

TO DRINK:
A light fruity red, like Côtes du Rhone from France

[Serves 4]

350g lean pork mince

350g lean beef mince

1 medium onion, cut into 5mm dice

1 tablespoon finely chopped garlic

2 tablespoons finely chopped fresh ginger

2 tablespoons Worcestershire sauce

1 tablespoon toasted sesame oil

180g 50-50 cooked White and Brown Rice (see page 12); save extra rice for another use

2 large eggs

sea salt and freshly ground black pepper

1 small head Chinese cabbage, cut into very thin strips

1 tablespoon sambal, for garnish

Ming's Tip:
To ease meatball making, wet your hands first.

TO DRINK:
An unoaked Chardonnay like
Elderton from the Barossa Valley
in Australia

[Serves 4]

1 banana leaf, 2 kale or iceberg lettuce
leaves or baking parchment cut to fit the
steamer top

four 175g thick salmon or arctic char fillets,
skin on

sea salt and freshly ground black pepper

1 tablespoon very thin strips peeled
fresh ginger

2 limes, halved and cut into 5mm-thick
half-moons

2 tablespoons naturally brewed soy sauce,
plus more for drizzling

4 tablespoons grapeseed or rapeseed oil

soy-lime steamed salmon with grapeseed oil flash

Finishing a dish with a drizzle of hot oil is an easy Chinese technique that gives steamed fish just the right touch of richness. Here, salmon (or use arctic char if you can find it) is steamed simply with lime slices, soy sauce and ginger, then finished with the oil. You get the clean tastiness of the fish, which couldn't be better for you, plus great flavour. The fillets are cooked skin on. The skin is nutritious, but you can remove it, if you like. I love my fish on the rare side, but if you don't, steam the fillets until just cooked through.

1. Set up a steamer. Place the banana leaf or other leaf or paper in the top part.

2. Season the fillets lightly with salt and pepper and transfer to the steamer skin side down. Sprinkle evenly with the ginger and top with the lime. Drizzle with the 2 tablespoons soy sauce and steam until the fillets are medium-rare, 8–10 minutes, or just cooked through, 10–12 minutes.

3. Meanwhile, in a small saucepan heat the oil to the smoking point. Very carefully, standing back to avoid splatters, use a tablespoon to spoon the hot oil over the cooked fillets in the steamer. If using a bamboo steamer, serve from it. Otherwise, transfer the fillets with the banana leaf, or alone if other leaves or baking parchment were used, to a platter. Drizzle with the soy sauce and serve.

Ming's Tip:

When shopping for fish, make sure to check it for absolute freshness. The fish should look naturally moist, without a bit of dryness. If whole, look for red gills, intact scales and no surface browning. No matter the cut, fish should smell fresh, like the sea. Ask your fish seller to put a potential purchase on a piece of paper so you can give it a sniff. If he or she objects, shop elsewhere!

flash-fried aubergine with honey-lemon syrup

TO DRINK:
Veuve Clicquot Champagne

[Serves 4]

1 large aubergine, cut into 5mm slices

sea salt and freshly ground black pepper

85g honey

1 tablespoon naturally brewed soy sauce

grated zest from 1 lemon, plus
1 tablespoon juice

5 spring onions, thinly sliced, white and green parts separated, 2 tablespoons of the greens reserved for garnish

2 large eggs

120g panko (Japanese breadcrumbs)

140g plain flour

grapeseed or rapeseed oil, for flash-frying

If you're a fan of aubergine –and even if you're not – you'll love this dish. Sliced thinly and flash-fried, aubergine is transformed into the best (not to mention largest) crisps you've ever had. Partnered by syrup inspired by the traditional Middle Eastern lemon and honey pairing, this starts any meal with a major bang.

1. Place the aubergine on a plate and salt generously. Leave to stand for 1 hour to release its liquid and any bitterness. Rinse well, pat dry, season with pepper and set aside.

2. In a small bowl, combine the honey, soy sauce, lemon zest and juice and the larger quantity of spring onion greens.

3. Beat the eggs in a large, shallow soup bowl. Combine the panko and spring onion whites on a large plate. Spread the flour on a second large plate. Dredge the aubergine in the flour, shake off any excess, dip it in the eggs and then dredge in the panko mixture.

4. Fill a large, high-sided frying pan with 1cm of the oil and heat over a medium heat to 180°C/350°F, as measured with a deep-fat thermometer. Working in batches, if necessary, fry the aubergine for 2–3 minutes until golden brown. Drain the aubergine on a kitchen paper-lined plate.

5. Stack the aubergine crisps on a serving plate, drizzle with the syrup, garnish with the remaining spring onion greens and serve.

TO DRINK:
A crisp lager like Yanjing
from China

[Serves 4]

2 tablespoons shiro miso

2 tablespoons naturally brewed ponzu,
plus more for drizzling

115g salted butter, at room temperature

grapeseed or rapeseed oil, for frying

two 350g packs silken tofu, each portion
quartered lengthways

1 tablespoon togarashi or chilli powder

sea salt and freshly ground black pepper

320g white rice flour

1/2 head iceberg lettuce, shredded

2 tablespoons finely sliced chives,
for garnish

crispy tofu with miso butter and iceberg lettuce

This recipe elevates humble yet healthful tofu to great, delicious heights. It's flash-fried, which makes it golden brown and crispy. The tofu's then dolloped with a flavourful miso butter whose richness is offset by ponzu and iceberg lettuce – a lettuce I've always loved for its compatible, no-frills crunchiness. This makes a great light meal or starter.

1. In a medium bowl, combine the miso and ponzu. Using a hand blender or sturdy whisk, whisk until well blended. Add the butter and whisk until blended. Set aside.

2. Fill a heavy medium frying pan 1cm full with the oil. Heat over a medium heat to 180°C/375°F.

3. Meanwhile, season the tofu with the togarashi and salt and pepper to taste. Spread the rice flour on a large plate, add the tofu and dredge on all sides. Shake off the excess flour and, using a skimmer or fish slice, transfer half the tofu to the oil. Fry the tofu until crisp, turning once, for 2–3 minutes. Drain on kitchen paper. Repeat with the remaining tofu.

4. Transfer the lettuce to a platter or divide the lettuce between four serving plates. Drizzle with the ponzu, top with the tofu and dollop with the butter mixture. Garnish with the chives and serve.

Ming's Tips:
The frying is best done in a heavy, straight-sided pan, but any heavy pan will do. You may have extra miso butter. Refrigerate it and use it later for searing fish or meat.

6

Soup is the ultimate one-pot dish – and undoubtedly the original. Its preparation is as basic as the satisfaction it delivers. You put ingredients in a pot, add liquid and simmer. Hours later – soup.

As easy as it is to prepare, though, there are soups and soups. I've made sure that the ones in this chapter, like Wonton Prawn and Noodle Soup and Beef and Onion 'Sukiyaki', are both convenient and delicious. Soups can be hearty and stew-like, such as Mussel and Rice Stew, or delicate and more dressed up, such as New-Style Halibut Sashimi Soup, a lovely, rave-getting starter. Soup is also one of the dishes most likely to make meat eaters shake hands with vegetarians: both will love my Five-Vegetable Miso Stew and Three Bean Chilli, as well as my takes on traditional favourites, like Lemongrass-Coconut Chicken Soup, based on the Thai *tom yung gai*, and Prawn Bouillabaisse. Soup is beloved by all – and one-pot easy too.

SOUP

lemongrass-coconut chicken soup

TO DRINK:
A full-bodied Sauvignon Blanc
from France

[Serves 4]

This light but deliciously fortifying soup is based on the Thai classic, *tom yung gai*. It features what I think of as the defining Thai flavouring, lemongrass, combined with chicken and coconut milk, and chillies for heat. I've followed the time-honoured Thai approach of leaving whole pieces of the lemongrass in the soup, but you can strain them out, if you like. (If you do leave them in, tell diners not to eat them.) This makes a great starter, of course, but is also terrific as a light meal accompanied by a salad dressed with citrus vinaigrette.

1. Heat a medium saucepan over a medium heat. Add the oil and swirl to coat the bottom. When the oil is hot, add the lemongrass and sauté, stirring, for 2 minutes. Add the celery, carrots, onions and chillies, if using, and sauté, stirring, for 1 minute. Season with salt and pepper.

2. Add the chicken and sauté for about 1 minute until opaque. Add the fish sauce and stock, stir, bring to a simmer and cook for about 5 minutes until the liquid is reduced by one fifth. Add the coconut milk and lemon juice and stir. Add the basil and adjust the seasoning, if necessary. Serve.

1 tablespoon grapeseed or rapeseed oil

4 lemongrass stalks, pale parts only, crushed with the flat side of a knife

1 head celery, sticks rinsed and roughly chopped

2 large carrots, peeled and shredded

2 medium onions, thinly sliced

2 bird's eye or serrano chillies, stems discarded and finely chopped (optional)

sea salt and freshly ground black pepper

2 boneless, skinless chicken breasts, cut widthways into 5mm strips

3 tablespoons Thai fish sauce

1.4 litres fresh chicken stock or stock made from low-salt chicken stock cubes

4 tablespoons coconut milk

juice of 1 lemon

small handful whole Thai basil leaves, or regular basil

beef and onion 'sukiyaki'

TO DRINK:
A clean Japanese beer like
Kirin, Saporo or Asahi

[Serves 4]

225g rice stick noodles

1 tablespoon grapeseed or rapeseed oil

3 large onions, halved and cut into
5mm slices

1 tablespoon finely chopped fresh ginger

125ml mirin

1.9 litres fresh chicken stock or stock made
from low-salt chicken stock cubes

2 tablespoons naturally brewed soy sauce

sea salt and freshly ground black pepper

450g beef fillet, sliced paper thinly
(see headnote)

This soupy, soul-satisfying dish is based on sukiyaki, a dish I first enjoyed in its home country, Japan. Like that dish, this one can be finished at the table, which makes it good for a special occasion, or for creating one. Here, paper-thin slices of beef – have your butcher do the cutting – are floated on the top of a steaming, noodle-filled broth, where they cook very quickly. You can substitute thinly sliced chicken for the beef, if you like, but whichever the meat, you'll enjoy a deliciously slurpy meal.

1. Place the noodles in a large bowl and cover them generously with hot water. Soak for about 20 minutes until soft. Drain and set aside.

2. Heat a large, deep frying pan over a high heat. Add the oil and swirl to coat the bottom. When the oil is hot, add the onions and ginger and sauté, stirring, for about 5 minutes until the onions have browned. Add the mirin, deglaze the pan and cook for about 3 minutes until reduced by one quarter. Add the stock, reduce the heat to medium and simmer for about 10 minutes until the liquid has reduced slightly. Add the noodles and soy sauce and season to taste with salt and pepper.

3. Using chopsticks or tongs, float the beef on the surface of the liquid until just cooked through, turning it once. It will be cooked in about 1 minute. Divide the beef, soup and noodles between heated bowls and serve with soup spoons and chopsticks.

Ming's Tip:

If you own a large, high-sided sauté pan – what the French call a 'sautoir' – you can cook the dish in it and bring it to the table.

miso butter pork
ramen noodle soup

TO DRINK:
A dry Japanese beer
like Kirin or Asahi

[Serves 4]

I grew up eating – and loving – Chinese noodle soups. Fast-forward to my culinary training in Japan, where I came to adore miso-flavoured broths with ramen noodles. My version borrows the hearty depth of those miso-laced soups and features the rich meatiness of pork. A bit of butter – definitely a Western touch – rounds everything out. I can't imagine an appetite this wouldn't satisfy, particularly on a cold day.

1. Fill a large bowl with water and add ice cubes. In a tall, wide saucepan, cook the noodles in abundant boiling salted water for 2–3 minutes if fresh or 6–8 minutes if dry. Drain the noodles and transfer to the iced water. When cold, drain and set aside.

2. Heat the same pan over a medium heat. Add the oil and swirl to coat the bottom. When the oil is hot, add the shallots, ginger and pork and sauté, breaking up the pork, for 3–4 minutes until the meat is cooked through. Add the spring onion whites and mirin, deglaze the pan and simmer for 1–2 minutes until the liquid is reduced by half. Add the stock and the apples and bring to a simmer.

3. Whisk in the butter and the miso and season with salt and pepper. Add the noodles and heat through for about 2 minutes. Divide the noodles and soup between four individual bowls, garnish with the spring onion greens and serve.

ice cubes

450g fresh or dried ramen noodles

sea salt

2 tablespoons grapeseed or rapeseed oil

3 shallots, finely chopped

1 tablespoon finely chopped fresh ginger

450g lean pork mince

1 bunch spring onions, thinly sliced, green and white parts separated

125ml mirin

1.9 litres fresh chicken stock or stock made from low-salt chicken stock cubes

2 Red Delicious apples, peeled, cored and thinly sliced

55g unsalted butter

6 tablespoons shiro miso

freshly ground black pepper

prawn bouillabaisse

TO DRINK:
A chilled rosé, like Tavel
from France

Traditional bouillabaisse is a marvellous dish that requires many kinds of seafood and a lot of time to make. My quicker version delivers all the thrills of the original but uses only prawns, plus fennel and edamame. Yogurt adds a sense of the characteristic creaminess, and buttery garlic bread completes the meal.

[Serves 4]

3 tablespoons grapeseed or rapeseed oil

675g uncooked medium prawns, peeled, deveined and halved lengthways, shells reserved

225ml dry white wine

1.9 litres fresh chicken stock or stock made from low-salt chicken stock cubes

sea salt and freshly ground black pepper

1 small fennel bulb, halved, cored and cut into 1cm dice

1 medium onion, cut into 5mm dice

1 large carrot, peeled and cut into 5mm dice

2 celery sticks, cut into 5mm dice

1 tablespoon paprika

150g shelled edamame

225ml Greek yogurt

55g unsalted butter, softened

1 tablespoon finely chopped garlic

1 baguette, cut on the bias into 1cm slices

1. Heat a tall, wide saucepan over a high heat. Add 2 tablespoons of the oil and swirl to coat the bottom. When the oil is hot, add the prawn shells and sauté, stirring, for 1–2 minutes until the shells have turned pink. Add the wine, deglaze the pan and simmer for 1–2 minutes until the liquid is reduced by half. Add the stock, season with salt and pepper and simmer for 5–6 minutes until the liquid is reduced by one quarter. Strain the liquid and transfer to a large bowl. Set aside. (Discard the shells.)

2. Preheat the grill. Dry out the pan and heat over a medium-high heat. Add the remaining tablespoon of oil and swirl to coat the bottom. When the oil is hot, add the fennel, onions, carrot, celery and paprika. Season with salt and pepper and sauté for about 3 minutes until the vegetables are soft. Add the strained stock, prawns and edamame and simmer for about 3 minutes until the prawns are just cooked through. Whisk in the yogurt and adjust the seasoning, if necessary.

3. Meanwhile, in a small bowl combine the butter and garlic. Season with salt and pepper, blend and spread on one side of the bread slices. Transfer to a large grill pan and grill at the middle level for 2–3 minutes until the bread is golden. Watch carefully to ensure that the bread doesn't burn.

4. Ladle the soup into four individual serving bowls and serve with the bread.

TO DRINK:
A Riesling from Germany

[Serves 4]

15g unsalted butter

2 tablespoons very fine strips peeled fresh ginger

1 medium onion, halved lengthways and thinly sliced

1 bunch spring onions, thinly sliced, white and green parts separated

sea salt and freshly ground black pepper

950ml fresh chicken stock or stock made from low-salt chicken stock cubes

one 115g piece halibut, cut into 5mm slices

pinches of togarashi (see page 11) or red chilli flakes, for garnish

2 sheets nori (dried seaweed), folded lengthways 6 times, then cut widthways with scissors into 3mm strips

new-style halibut sashimi soup

This is by far the lightest and most delicate recipe in this book – and a fantastic way to start a meal. You make a delicious broth that's topped by pristine slices of raw halibut. The halibut is partially cooked by the hot liquid, and it retains the texture of sashimi. Ribbons of nori and a sprinkling of chilli flakes complete the presentation, which is especially memorable if you do the final soup-ladling at the table.

1. Heat a large saucepan over a low heat. Add the butter, and when hot, add the ginger, onions and spring onion whites. Sauté, stirring, for 1–2 minutes until soft. Season with salt and pepper. Add the stock and bring to a simmer. Reduce the heat and simmer for 3–4 minutes until the stock is reduced by one quarter.

2. Using a skimmer, remove the onions and ginger from the stock and transfer to four individual serving bowls. Top each with the halibut slices. Sprinkle with the togarashi, spring onion greens and nori. Ladle in the broth until it just covers the fish (or for cooked-through fish, cover it with broth) and serve immediately.

Ming's Tip:

To make this dish a success, as well as healthful eating, you must get absolutely fresh, sashimi-grade fish. Once that's taken care of, you'll have a fantastic dish that's also quick to do.

TO DRINK:
An unoaked Chablis-like
Chardonnay from California

[Serves 4]

1 tablespoon grapeseed or rapeseed oil

8 garlic cloves, thinly sliced

2 shallots, thinly sliced

2 rashers back bacon, cut into 5mm dice

1 large fennel bulb, halved, cored and sliced
5mm thick

450g live mussels, cleaned and debearded

475ml dry white wine

475ml fresh chicken stock or stock made
from a low-salt chicken stock cube

360g 50-50 cooked White and Brown
Rice (see page 12); save extra rice for
another use

1 tablespoon oyster sauce, vegetarian oyster
sauce or wheat-free tamari sauce

sea salt and freshly ground black pepper

1 lemon, quartered, for garnish

mussel and
rice stew

Different cultures have different takes on breakfast. A traditional Chinese breakfast consists of jook, which is a rice porridge, with all kinds of savoury additions, including meat and fish. You might call this 'super-jook' as it's made with a brown rice mixture, stock and mussels, plus bacon. You could serve this for breakfast, but it's really meant for later in the day, when you want something comforting after long hours at work.

1. Heat a tall, wide saucepan over a high heat. Add the oil and swirl to coat the bottom. When the oil is hot, add the garlic, shallots, bacon and fennel and sauté, stirring, for about 3 minutes until the vegetables are soft. Add the mussels and heat through, stirring, for 2 minutes Add the wine, deglaze the pan and simmer for about 3 minutes until the liquid is reduced by half. Remove any mussels that haven't opened and discard. Transfer the mussels to a bowl and set aside.

2. Add the stock, rice and oyster sauce to the pan. Bring to a simmer and cook for 15–20 minutes until the rice has released its starch and the mixture is stew-like. Return the mussels to the pan, heat through and season with salt and pepper. Transfer the soup to four individual serving bowls and distribute the mussels in each. Serve with the lemon wedges.

wonton prawn and noodle soup

Wonton soup is a great favourite, but is laborious to prepare at home, as the wontons must be made from scratch. For this delicious, easier version, wontons are replaced by wonton noodles – thin egg pasta. You get satisfying noodle slurp as well as a rich, prawn-filled broth. I sometimes add handfuls of baby spinach leaves or julienned bok choy to the soup, but it's delicious as it is.

1. Fill a large bowl with water and add ice cubes. In a tall, wide saucepan, cook the noodles in abundant boiling salted water for about 3 minutes until al dente. Drain the noodles and transfer to the iced water. When cold, drain and transfer to a medium bowl. Drizzle in oil to coat the noodles lightly and set aside.

2. Heat the pan over a high heat. Add the oil and swirl to coat the bottom. When the oil is hot, add the spring onion whites, the larger quantity of the greens, ginger and star anise and sauté for about 1 minute until softened. Add the stock, bring to a simmer and cook for about 5 minutes until reduced by one quarter. Add the soy sauce, sesame oil, carrots, noodles and prawns. Simmer for about 3 minutes until the prawns are just cooked through.

3. Transfer to four individual soup bowls, garnish with the remaining spring onion greens and serve.

TO DRINK:
Green tea with toasted brown rice

[Serves 4]

ice cubes

225g wonton noodles or angel hair pasta

sea salt

1 tablespoon grapeseed or rapeseed oil, plus more for coating the noodles

2 bunches spring onions, thinly sliced, white and green parts separated, 50g greens reserved for garnish

1 tablespoon thinly sliced fresh ginger

1 star anise

1.9 litres fresh chicken stock or stock made from low-salt chicken stock cubes

2 tablespoons naturally brewed soy sauce

1 tablespoon toasted sesame oil

135g carrots, peeled and shredded

450g small, uncooked peeled prawns

spicy clam
and prawn soup

This light but deeply flavourful soup borrows from the Thai storecupboard by using lemongrass, chillies, lime and coconut milk. I've upped the ante, though, by adding clams and prawns, whose briny sweetness is heightened by the other flavourings. Thai basil adds its own liquorice-like appeal. Before cooking, the clams are purged, an unattended soaking process that ensures grit-free eating. If, however, you don't have the time and don't mind the possibility of a bit of grit, you can skip it.

1. Fill a large bowl with water. Add the polenta, stir and add the clams. Leave the clams to purge for at least 1 hour and up to 3.

2. Meanwhile, heat a tall, wide saucepan over a medium heat. Add the oil and swirl to coat the bottom. When the oil is hot, add the shallots, chillies, ginger, lime leaves and lemongrass and sauté, stirring, for 1 minute. Add the clams, season lightly with salt and pepper and cook, stirring occasionally, for 2–3 minutes until the clams start to open. Deglaze with the fish sauce and lime juice.

3. Add the chicken stock and basil sprigs, cover and bring to a simmer. Cook for 4–5 minutes until the clams have opened fully (discard any clams that haven't opened). Add the prawns and coconut milk and simmer for about 3 minutes until the prawns are cooked through. Transfer to four individual bowls, garnish with the basil leaves and serve.

TO DRINK:
An off-dry Gewürztraminer
from Germany

[Serves 4]

35g polenta

450g live clams or cockles

1 tablespoon grapeseed or rapeseed oil

4 shallots, thinly sliced

2 bird's eye chillies, dseeded and thinly sliced

two 5mm-thick slices fresh ginger cut from a 5–10cm piece

6 Kaffir lime leaves, hand-crushed

2 lemongrass stalks, white part only, crushed with the flat of a knife

sea salt and freshly ground black pepper

2 tablespoons fish sauce

juice of 4 limes

1.9 litres fresh chicken stock or stock made from low-salt chicken stock cubes

4 sprigs Thai basil, plus 8 leaves for garnish

225g small, uncooked peeled prawns

4 tablespoons coconut milk

Ming's Tip:

If any clams refuse to open after full cooking, throw them away. But those that open slightly can be coaxed to open further, and therefore be used, by inserting the tip of a spoon between the shells and prying gently.

vegetarian hot and sour soup

You don't need pork to make a fabulous hot and sour soup. The secret is having a deeply flavoured broth, which you definitely get in this meatless version. You also get three layers of heat, supplied by ginger, jalapeños and white pepper. Very quickly prepared, this makes a bracing starter guaranteed to whet appetites.

1. Heat a tall, wide saucepan over a high heat. Add the oil and swirl to coat the bottom. When the oil is hot, add the spring onion whites, chillies and ginger and sauté, stirring, for 1 minute until softened. Add the white pepper, vinegar, soy sauce and stock and bring to a simmer.

2. Add the tofu and enoki and season with more pepper. Transfer the soup to four individual serving bowls, garnish with the spring onion greens and serve.

TO DRINK:
A Gewürztraminer, like Zind Humbrecht from France

[Serves 4]

1 tablespoon grapeseed or rapeseed oil

2 bunches spring onions, thinly sliced, white and green parts separated

2 jalapeño chillies, thinly sliced

2 tablespoons thinly sliced peeled fresh ginger

2 teaspoons finely ground white pepper, plus more

125ml naturally brewed rice vinegar

6 tablespoons naturally brewed soy sauce

1.9 litres vegetable stock

two 350g packs silken tofu, cut lengthways into 5mm x 5mm strips

200–225g enoki mushrooms, ends trimmed

TO DRINK:
Sencha green tea

five-vegetable miso stew

Choosing to use miso as the flavour base of this delicious stew was a no-brainer. Miso provides as much deep flavour as a meat addition might, and is way better for you. Sweet potatoes, kale, tomatoes and a touch of tamari do the rest. Vegetable stews can be boring, but this one is a second-helping treat.

[Serves 4]

2 tablespoons grapeseed or rapeseed oil

1 bunch spring onions, thinly sliced, green and white parts separated

1 large onion, finely chopped

1 large sweet potato, cut into 1cm dice

sea salt and freshly ground black pepper

1 tablespoon finely chopped fresh ginger

500g canned whole Italian plum tomatoes, roughly chopped, with the juice from measuring

1.9 litres vegetable stock

1 tablespoon wheat-free tamari sauce

6 tablespoons miso

200g (prepared weight) curly kale leaves, stems discarded and cut into 5mm strips

extra-virgin olive oil, for drizzling

2 wholemeal pitta breads, toasted and quartered

1. Heat a tall, wide saucepan over a medium heat. Add the oil and swirl to coat the bottom. When the oil is hot, add the spring onion whites, onions and potatoes, season with salt and pepper and sauté for about 5 minutes until the onions have browned lightly. Add the ginger, tomatoes with their juice, stock and tamari.

2. Place the miso in a small sieve, submerge it in the pan and whisk it until it has dispersed into the liquid, then remove the sieve. Adjust the seasoning, if necessary. Bring the stew to a simmer and cook for about 10 minutes until the potatoes are soft and the liquid is reduced by a quarter. Adjust the seasoning again, if necessary.

3. Add the kale and simmer for 1–2 minutes until soft. Taste the seasoning a final time and adjust, if necessary.

4. Transfer the stew to four individual soup bowls. Drizzle with the olive oil and serve with the pitta.

three-bean chilli

Every Halloween I make a huge pot of chilli to serve to parents who arrive at our door with their kids – or is it the other way around? This meatless update packs serious flavour because of the fermented black beans and tamari in it, plus there's edamame and white and black beans – not only tasty, but good for you. Also included: chilli heat in abundance.

1. Heat a tall, wide saucepan over a medium-high heat. Add the oil and swirl to coat the bottom. When the oil is hot, add the onions, garlic, fermented black beans, chillies and spring onion whites. Sauté for 4–5 minutes until lightly caramelised. Add the tamari sauce and deglaze the pan. Add the edamame, the white and black beans, tomatoes with their juice and stock and bring to a simmer. Add the lemon juice and season with salt and pepper. Simmer for 45–60 minutes until the mixture has reduced by one quarter.

2. Meanwhile, in a small bowl, combine the yogurt, spring onion greens and lemon zest. Season with salt and pepper. Serve from the pan or transfer the chilli to four individual serving bowls. Serve with the yogurt on the side.

TO DRINK:
Chilled beer, like Yanjing from China or Samuel Adams

[Serves 4]

2 tablespoons grapeseed or rapeseed oil

2 medium red onions, cut into 4mm dice

2 tablespoons finely chopped garlic

2 tablespoons fermented black beans

2 serrano chillies, finely chopped

1 bunch spring onions, thinly sliced, green and white parts separated

4 tablespoons wheat-free tamari sauce

300g shelled edamame

one 400g can haricot or cannellini beans, rinsed and drained

two 400g cans black beans, rinsed and drained

500g canned whole Italian plum tomatoes, roughly chopped, with the juice from measuring

950ml vegetable stock or unsweetened black tea

juice and grated zest of 1 lemon

sea salt and freshly ground black pepper

225ml Greek yogurt

Ming's Tip:

I always make extra chili because it's one of those dishes that tastes even better the next day, and better still the day after.

7

Once I saw salads as 'one-pot' dishes – they're tossed and served in the same bowl – I recognised how convenient they can be. A good thing, because salads are extremely versatile and fill many menu slots. Salads were formerly understood to be 'small-plate' dishes only. We now enjoy a vast range of main course salads, which can be easy and fun to put together. The recipes in this chapter showcase these meal-in-one salads – whether they are recastings of traditional dishes, such as Coriander-Crusted Tuna Salad Niçoise and Tofu Green Goddess Salad, or delicious 'inventions' like Spicy Prawn and Avocado Salad.

I've also enjoyed lightening favourite salads that relied, usually, on a mayo-based dressing. In place of mayo, I use good-for-you Greek yogurt, which provides creaminess without any heaviness. My Seared Salmon and Greek Yogurt Salad headlines the technique. And for special occasions, I offer Tea-Smoked Salmon with Preserved Lemon and Fennel-Couscous Salad, which may sound like a big deal to put together, but it isn't. My one-pot approach gives salads a new – and really convenient -- lease on life.

TOSS

sesame chicken cucumber noodle salad

TO DRINK:
A bright, exotic-fruit Sauvignon Blanc, like a Mulderbosch from South Africa

[Serves 4]

Just about everyone loves sesame noodle salad, including me. This delicious version improves on the traditional one because it uses a mixture of creamy peanut butter and sesame oil in place of the customary sesame paste. The resulting dish is lighter, not only because the noodles are more delicately coated with the dressing, but because there's less of them in relation to the chicken and veggies.

1. Fill a large bowl with water and add ice cubes. Cook the noodles in abundant boiling salted water until al dente: 2–4 minutes if fresh, about 6 minutes or according to the packet instructions if dry. Drain and transfer to the iced water. When the noodles are cold, drain and coat lightly with vegetable oil. Set aside.

2. If using baby cos lettuce, half lengthways, notch out the core and then cut widthways into 1cm pieces. If using regular cos, remove the tougher outer leaves. Halve lengthways, notch out the core, halve again and cut widthways into 1cm pieces. Set aside.

3. For the dressing, in a large bowl whisk together the peanut butter, sesame oil, vinegar and wine. Add the spring onions, sambal, soy sauce and coriander, if using, and stir to blend. Transfer the dressing to a small bowl.

4. In the first bowl, combine the chicken, cucumber, red peppers, lettuce and noodles. Add three quarters of the dressing and toss. Season with salt and black pepper. Add the remaining dressing, if necessary.

5. Transfer the salad to a serving bowl. Garnish with the sesame seeds and serve.

Ming's Tip:

I always cook extra noodles when making this dish. Cooked noodles, stored in the refrigerator, can be turned rapidly into a tasty pan-fried noodle cake or chow mein.

ice cubes

225g Chinese egg noodles or other thin noodles or pasta, fresh or dried

sea salt

vegetable oil, for coating the pasta

2 heads baby cos or 1 head regular cos lettuce

260g creamy peanut butter

2 tablespoons toasted sesame oil

175ml naturally brewed rice vinegar

2 tablespoons Shaoxing wine or dry sherry

100g spring onions, thinly sliced, white and green parts

1 tablespoon sambal, any kind, or hot sauce

2 tablespoons naturally brewed soy sauce

4 tablespoons chopped fresh coriander (optional)

3 large cooked boneless, skinless chicken breasts (about 675g), cut lengthways into 5mm slices and chilled

1 large cucumber, peeled, deseeded, halved lengthways and cut into 5mm slices

2 medium red peppers, deseeded and cut into 5mm dice

freshly ground black pepper

toasted sesame seeds, for garnish

tamari-shallot chicken frisée salad

TO DRINK:
A Spanish Verdejo

[Serves 4]

4 boneless, skinless medium chicken breasts (about 900g)

sea salt and freshly ground black pepper

non-stick cooking spray or vegetable oil, for oiling the barbecue rack

2 tablespoons grapeseed or rapeseed oil, if needed, plus 4 tablespoons grapeseed oil for the vinaigrette

2 large shallots, finely chopped

2 tablespoons wheat-free tamari sauce

4 tablespoons naturally brewed ponzu

1 tablespoon toasted sesame oil

1 bunch radishes, thinly sliced

150g shelled edamame

1 large head frisée, washed, cored and leaves halved

Everyone loves chicken salad, a dish you don't see enough of. My version takes a fresh approach and is also hassle-free. Here, the chicken is barbecued and accompanied by a frisée salad featuring, among other things, the fresh, crispy bitterness of radishes plus the creamy-crunchy bite of edamame. This makes a great picnic or patio dish.

1. Season the chicken with salt and pepper. Preheat a gas barbecue to high for 10 minutes. Standing back, spray the rack carefully with non-stick cooking spray (or rub quickly with kitchen paper blotted in vegetable oil). Cook the chicken, turning once, for 10–12 minutes until cooked through. Alternatively, heat a large griddle pan or heavy frying pan over a medium-high heat. Add the 2 tablespoons oil and swirl to coat the bottom. When the oil is hot, add the chicken and sauté, turning once, for 10–12 minutes until cooked through. Remove the chicken to a chopping board and leave to rest for 5 minutes. Cut the chicken into 5mm slices and set aside.

2. Meanwhile, in a large bowl, combine the shallots, tamari and ponzu. Whisk in the 4 tablespoons grapeseed oil and the sesame oil. Transfer to a small bowl.

3. In the first bowl, combine the radishes, edamame and frisée with three quarters of the vinaigrette. Season with salt and pepper. Divide the salad between four individual plates, top with the chicken, drizzle with the remaining vinaigrette and serve.

warm lemongrass chicken with olive and cucumber-couscous salad

TO DRINK:
A fragrant Spanish white wine,
like Botani Moscatel Seco

Preserved lemons are often paired with couscous in Morocco, from where couscous originated. For this delicious salad I use lemongrass in place of the fruit, a subtlety boost, and add super-healthy cucumber for its crunch and colour. Seared marinated chicken breasts complete the delicious meal.

1. Season the chicken with salt and pepper on both sides. In a large resealable plastic bag, combine the lemongrass, shallots, wine and 2 tablespoons of the oil. Add the chicken breasts, seal the bag and, using your hands, evenly distribute the marinade. Leave to marinate for 30 minutes at room temperature.

2. Transfer the chicken to a plate and reserve the marinade. Season the chicken again with salt and pepper on both sides.

3. Heat a large frying over a medium heat. Add 2 more tablespoons of the oil and swirl to coat the bottom. When the oil is hot, add the chicken and sauté, turning once, for 8–10 minutes until browned and cooked through. Transfer the chicken to a plate, leave to rest for 10 minutes and set aside.

4. Make the couscous by bringing a generous 1 litre water to the boil in a medium saucepan. Add the couscous, drizzle with 1 tablespoon of the oil and stir. Remove from the heat, cover and leave to stand for 4–5 minutes until the couscous has absorbed the water. Fluff up with a fork, season with salt and pepper, stir gently to blend and set aside.

5. Add the reserved marinade to the frying pan and bring to a simmer. Add the olives, cucumber, lemon juice and the remaining 4 tablespoons oil. Season with salt and pepper, stir and heat through for 1–2 minutes.

6. Meanwhile, slice the chicken 5mm thick and return it to the pan. Transfer the couscous to a serving bowl, top with the pan mixture, garnish with the lemon zest and serve.

[Serves 4]

3 boneless, skinless chicken breasts (about 675g pounds)

sea salt and freshly ground black pepper

5 lemongrass stalks, white part only, finely chopped (see Ming's Tip, page 66)

3 shallots, finely chopped

125ml dry white wine

9 tablespoons extra-virgin olive oil

525g couscous

45g pitted Niçoise olives, chopped

1 cucumber, cut into 5mm dice

juice and grated zest of 1 lemon

sesame-crusted salmon with miso-shallot salad

TO DRINK:
A buttery California Chardonnay, like Newton Unfiltered

[Serves 4]

I devised the salad for this dish after enjoying a classic Japanese vinaigrette, which is made from miso plus onion. Shallots, with their hint of garlic, are a better onion for the job and, combined with the miso, create a vinaigrette of delicious depth. The sesame seeds add not only crunch to the salmon but also a tasty nuttiness.

4 tablespoons shiro miso

2 large shallots, roughly chopped

1 teaspoon togarashi or red chilli flakes

1 tablespoon sugar

juice of 2 lemons

4 tablespoons ponzu or naturally brewed rice vinegar

1 teaspoon toasted sesame oil

225ml grapeseed or rapeseed oil, plus 1 tablespoon for the pan

sea salt and freshly ground black pepper

four 175–225g skinless salmon fillets

110g untoasted sesame seeds

115g rocket, washed and well dried

150g cherry tomatoes, halved

1. In a blender, combine the miso, shallots, togarashi, sugar, lemon juice, ponzu and sesame oil and blend on high speed until smooth. With the blender still running, slowly drizzle in the 225ml grapeseed oil. Season with salt and pepper. Transfer half to a jug and set aside. (Store the rest in an airtight container, refrigerated, for later use. It will last up to a week.)

2. Season the salmon with salt and pepper on both sides. Place the sesame seeds on a large plate and press the salmon into them on both sides.

3. Add the 1 tablespoon oil to a large non-stick sauté pan, swirl to coat the bottom and heat over a medium-high heat. When the oil is hot, add the salmon and sauté, turning once, for 4 minutes until the salmon is rare, or 8–10 minutes until cooked through. (If the sesame seeds seem to be browning too quickly, turn the fillets on their sides; they'll continue to cook.) Transfer the salmon to a chopping board and cut it into 5mm slices.

4. In a large bowl, combine the rocket, tomatoes and 5 tablespoons of the miso vinaigrette and toss. Transfer the salad to a platter or divide between four individual serving plates. Top with the salmon, drizzle on additional vinaigrette and serve.

Ming's Tip:

To make blending possible, this recipe yields twice the vinaigrette it requires. But you'll definitely want extra to have on hand to toss with other salads. For that reason, I always recommend making double quantities of vinaigrette.

coriander-crusted tuna salad niçoise

I've always enjoyed composed salads – salads with multiple ingredients artfully arranged. Among these, salade Niçoise is probably the best known and most widely enjoyed. It features tuna – traditionally, canned albacore. I've 'upped' the dish by using fresh, coriander-coated tuna that's quickly sautéed, plus frisée dressed with a sprightly caper-and-olive-laced vinaigrette. This is a great outdoor dish, perfect for a summer lunch.

1. To hard-boil the eggs, bring enough water to cover the eggs to the boil in a medium saucepan. Lower the eggs into the water and immediately reduce the heat to a simmer. Simmer for 14 minutes and then transfer the eggs to cold water. When cold, peel and slice the eggs 5mm thick. Set aside.

2. Make the vinaigrette. In a small bowl combine the mustard, shallots, ponzu, sesame oil, capers and olives and whisk to blend. Slowly whisk in the 125ml olive oil and season with salt and pepper. Set aside.

3. Season the tuna with salt and pepper on both sides. Spread the coriander on a large plate and press the tuna into it on all sides.

4. Heat a medium sauté pan over a medium-high heat. Make sure the pan is very hot. Add the 1 tablespoon olive oil and swirl to coat the bottom. When the oil is hot, add the tuna and sauté on all sides for about 4 minutes until medium-rare. Remove the tuna and set aside.

5. In a large bowl, combine the frisée and eggs. Season with salt and pepper. Toss gently with the vinaigrette, reserving some for drizzling.

6. Divide the salad between four individual serving plates, top with the tuna, drizzle with the remaining vinaigrette and serve.

TO DRINK:
A crisp, fruit-forward Sancerre like Lucien Crochet from France

[Serves 4]

2 large eggs

2 tablespoons Dijon mustard

2 tablespoons finely chopped shallots

4 tablespoons naturally brewed ponzu

1 tablespoon toasted sesame oil

2 tablespoons chopped capers

2 tablespoons chopped pitted Niçoise olives

125ml plus 1 tablespoon extra-virgin olive oil

sea salt and freshly ground black pepper

450g centre-cut fresh tuna steak, cut lengthways into slices as wide as the tuna's thickness and as long as the steak

3 tablespoons coarsely ground coriander seeds (see Ming's Tip, page 107)

2 small heads frisée lettuce, washed, cored and cut into bite-sized pieces

Ming's Tip:

Wash the lettuce in the basket of a salad spinner plunged into a sinkful of cold water, drain it and then spin dry. You can store the lettuce – or any lettuce you want to use later – in the basket in the fridge.

TO DRINK:
A crisp Viognier, like Fairview
from South Africa

[Serves 4]

475ml Greek yogurt

2 large shallots, finely chopped

4 tablespoons thinly sliced mint leaves, plus
8 leaves for garnish

2 large tomatoes, cut into 1cm dice

sea salt and freshly ground black pepper

four 2.5cm-thick slices country bread or
other crusty bread

1 small head iceberg lettuce, shredded

2 tablespoons extra-virgin olive oil

675g skinless salmon fillet, cut
into 1cm slices

seared salmon and greek yogurt salad

I love salmon paired with bread and salad. For this all-in-one recipe, seared salmon is served atop lettuce-covered crusty bread and is dressed with mint-and-tomato-laced Greek yogurt. Greek yogurt is my favourite option for providing creaminess that's also refreshing. Besides being delicious, this dish is also perfect for those who worry about not cooking fish properly. With a quick sauté, it's just about impossible to undercook the salmon, which is always moist and succulent when served. This is put together so quickly, you'll make it part of your weekday dish rotation.

1. In a medium bowl, combine the yogurt, shallots, mint and tomatoes and stir gently to blend. Season with salt and pepper. Set aside.

2. Divide the bread between four individual serving plates. Top with the lettuce and set aside.

3. Heat a medium sauté pan over a medium heat. Add 1 tablespoon of the oil, and when hot, add half the salmon. Season the salmon with salt and pepper and sauté, turning once, for about 2 minutes until just cooked through. Transfer the salmon to two of the plates, add the remaining tablespoon of oil to the pan and sauté the remaining salmon. Transfer to the other two plates.

4. Spoon the yogurt mixture on top of the salmon fillets, garnish with the mint leaves and serve immediately.

TO DRINK:
A chilled Junmai Ginjo sake

tea-smoked salmon with preserved lemon and fennel-couscous salad

Tea-smoked salmon is a great treat. I do my own version using a tea and spice rub, but the salmon is also available already prepared in some speciality shops and online. You can, however, use any best-quality smoked salmon for this delicious salad, which balances the rich fish with two levels of lively flavour: preserved lemon and fennel. Couscous adds its own satisfying bite.

[Serves 4]

175g couscous

3 tablespoons extra-virgin olive oil, plus more for oiling and drizzling

10g thinly sliced chives

sea salt and freshly ground black pepper

225g tea-smoked salmon slices, or other high-quality smoked salmon

3¹/₂ tablespoons finely chopped preserved lemon

1 large fennel bulb, halved, cored and thinly sliced, fronds reserved for garnish

juice of 1 lemon

1 small courgette, cut into 3mm dice

1 tablespoon finely chopped tarragon

1. To make the couscous, bring 350ml water to the boil in a medium saucepan. Add the couscous, drizzle with 1 tablespoon of the oil and stir. Remove from the heat, cover and leave to stand for 4–5 minutes until the couscous has absorbed the water. Fluff up with a fork, add the chives and season with salt and pepper. Stir gently to blend and set aside.

2. Divide the salmon slices between 4 large salad plates, arranging it as you would carpaccio.

3. In a medium bowl, combine the preserved lemon, fennel, lemon juice, courgette, tarragon and the remaining 2 tablespoons of oil. Season with salt and pepper and stir to blend.

4. Coat four small bowls or ramekins lightly with oil. Divide the fennel salad between the moulds and press firmly. Top with the couscous and pack firmly with the back of a spoon. Invert the moulds to the side of the salmon, drizzle with oil, garnish with the fennel fronds and serve.

spicy prawn and avocado salad

I got the idea for this delicious salad after enjoying ceviche with avocado and peppers, a traditional Latin American pairing. Here, prawns are quickly sautéed, combined with avocado, red pepper and jicama and served simply atop lettuce with toasted pitta bread. That's it – a definite example of less being more.

1. Heat a medium sauté pan over a medium heat. Add the 2 tablespoons oil and swirl to coat the bottom. When the oil is hot, add the onion and jalapeño and sauté, stirring, for about 1 minute until the onions have softened. Season with salt and pepper. Add the prawns and sauté for about 4 mintues until just cooked through. Adjust the seasoning and transfer everything to a medium bowl.

2. Add the jicama, red pepper, avocados and lime juice and season with salt and pepper. Toss gently.

3. Toast and quarter the pitta, drizzle with olive oil and sprinkle with salt. Divide the lettuce leaves between four individual plates. Top with the prawn mixture. Arrange the pitta around the salad, garnish the salad with chives and serve.

TO DRINK:
A sparkling wine from Spain, like Brut Cava

[Serves 4]

2 tablespoons extra-virgin olive oil, plus more for drizzling

1 small red onion, finely chopped

1 jalapeño chilli, finely chopped

sea salt and freshly ground black pepper

450g small, uncooked peeled prawns

1 small jicama, cut into 5mm dice

1 medium red pepper, deseeded and cut into 5mm dice

2 avocados, stoned, peeled and cut into 1cm dice

juice of 2 limes

4 pieces wholemeal pitta bread

leaves from 1 head looseleaf lettuce

1 tablespoon thinly sliced chives

Ming's Tip:
Use a toaster to toast the pitta.

tofu greek salad

Greek salad is one of those classic dishes that travels far beyond its country of origin. As much as I enjoy it, I figured that there was a different, more refined way to approach it. My version is most deliciously notable for its substitution of firm tofu for the usual salty feta. Believe me, there's no flavour sacrifice, as I've also included fermented black beans and garlic in the dressing.

1. Heat a medium sauté pan over a medium-high heat. Add 4 tablespoons of the oil and swirl to coat the bottom. When the oil is hot, add the spring onion whites, garlic and beans and sauté, stirring, for about 1 minute until softened. Add the tomatoes and sauté for about 3 mintues until softened.

2. In a medium bowl, combine the mustard and lemon juice, the remaining oil, the parsley and the olives. Add the tomato mixture and cos lettuce and toss gently to combine. Season with salt and pepper. Add the tofu and toss gently again. Garnish with the lemon zest and serve.

TO DRINK:
A crisp Californian Sauvignon Blanc

[Serves 4]

125ml extra-virgin olive oil

1 bunch spring onions, thinly sliced, white and green parts separated

1 tablespoon finely chopped garlic

1 tablespoon finely chopped fermented black beans

150g cherry tomatoes, halved

2 tablespoons Dijon mustard

juice and grated zest of 1 lemon

25g flat-leaf parsley leaves

45g pitted Niçose olives, chopped

1 large head cos lettuce, tough outer leaves removed, cored, halved and cut widthways into 2.5cm pieces

sea salt and freshly ground black pepper

one 400g packet firm tofu, cut into 1cm dice

tofu green goddess salad

[Serves 4]

6 rashers streaky bacon

3 ripe avocados, stoned, peeled and roughly chopped

1 bunch spring onions, thinly sliced, white and green parts separated

15g flat-leaf parsley leaves

juice of 3 limes

sea salt and freshly ground black pepper

4 tablespoons extra-virgin olive oil

–

1 head iceberg lettuce, washed, cored and cut into 2.5cm pieces, 70g set aside

3 tomatoes, cut into 5mm slices

3 hard-boiled eggs, sliced 5mm thick

260g frozen peas, rinsed in hot water and drained, 35g set aside for garnish

one 350g pack silken tofu, cut lengthways into 5mm slices

Ming's Tip:

If you can get really fresh peas, by all means use them. Otherwise, frozen peas work beautifully.

Layered salads were part of my growing up in Ohio. Though I don't recall any made with green goddess dressing – a tarragon- and anchovy-spiked mayonnaise blend – mayo was a constant. This lighter version features tofu in place of the mayo, plus avocado, which ensures creaminess. The salad is layered in a bowl and unmoulded – a pretty, as well as mouthwatering, presentation.

1. In a medium frying pan, cook the bacon over a medium-low heat for about 8 minutes until crisp. Drain on kitchen paper, roughly chop and set aside.

2. To make the dressing, combine the avocados, spring onion whites, parsley and lime juice in a food processor and purée. Season with salt and pepper. With the processor running, drizzle in the oil. Adjust the seasoning, if necessary.

3. In a small bowl, combine the 70g lettuce with 2 tablespoons of the dressing, toss and set aside. Reserve 4 tablespoons of the dressing for garnish.

4. To make the salad, in a large salad bowl layer as follows (seasoning with salt and pepper, and spooning on some of the larger quantity of dressing between the layers): tomatoes, eggs, peas, tofu, bacon, dressed and undressed lettuce. Press down gently with a hand or large spoon to compress and refrigerate for 30 minutes.

5. Unmould the salad on a large round platter. Garnish with the reserved dressing, the spring greens and reserved peas and serve.

Acknowledgements
Both authors would like to thank Kyle Cathie, and US publisher and editor Anja Schmidt for her passion for perfection. Working with her has been a joy.

Ming Tsai
Many thanks to chefs Joanne O'Connell and Denise Swidey, who did an amazing job at a furious pace for this book. Thanks also to the entire Blue Ginger crew, led by Jonathan Taylor, Tom Woods, Jonathan Donoghue, Myron Chinn and Mario Solis, and to Michele Fadden and Deanne Steffen. My gratitude as well to Blue Ginger managers Paula Taylor, Deborah Blish, Dan Adelson and Erika Staaf.

My thanks also for the great assistance provided by Jill Hardy and Lisa Falso – for their help with all logistics and props, not to mention the 5-Hour Energy shots! And gratitude to Melissa's/World Variety Produce, Inc, Captain Marden's Seafoods, T F Kinnealey & Co and John Dewar and Company for their ongoing support and for providing their superior products for the shoot.

To the amazing photographer Antonis Achilleos, assisted by Christopher Coppa, many thanks for his beautiful, elegant photos.

Thanks also to Sandy Montag, my agent at IMG, for all you've done. And thanks to my writer extraordinaire, Arthur Boehm. This is our third book, Artie, but definitely not our last!

Arthur Boehm
Thanks, first, to Ming Tsai, for his wonderful food and the pleasure of writing about it this third time. Many thanks also to my agent, Joy Tutela of David Black Literary Agency, for her warmly attentive professionalism. Gratitude, too, to Lisa Falso for her generous help in preparing the recipes for publication. And many kisses to Tama Starr for her friendship and support in so many ways – then, now and, with any luck, always.

THANKS